TO SHARE WITH GOD'S POOR

TO SHARE WITH GOD'S POOR

SISTER AMONG THE OUTCASTS

Sister Emmanuelle Cinquin

Translated by Kathryn Spink

With Introduction and Photographs by Hilary Weir

1817

HARPER & ROW, PUBLISHERS, San Francisco
Cambridge, Hagerstown, New York, Philadelphia
London, Mexico City, São Paulo, Sydney

Translated from the original French edition, *Chiffonnière avec les Chiffonniers*, copyright © 1977 by Les Editions Ouvrières, Paris.

This English translation originally published by Triangle/SPCK, London, under the title *Sister with the Ragpickers*, 1982.

FIRST U.S. EDITION

Library of Congress Cataloging in Publication Data

Cinquin, Emmanuelle.
  TO SHARE WITH GOD'S POOR.

  Translation of: Chiffonnière avec les chiffonniers.
  British ed. published as: Sister with the ragpickers.
  1. Cinquin, Emmanuelle. 2. Nuns—Egypt—Cairo—Biography. 3. Cairo (Egypt)—Biography. I. Title.
BX4705.C5435A3313 1983   271'.9 [B]   83-47735
ISBN 0-06-061392-0

83 84 85 86 87 10 9 8 7 6 5 4 3 2 1

Contents

Introduction

The ragpickers of this book, in Arabic *zabbaleen*, are the unmentionables of Cairo. *Zabbal* means dung; *zabbaleen* the people who collect it. The English terms sum up society's view of this trade and its practitioners: rubbish, beneath notice. Until Sister Emmanuelle came to their aid in 1971, the *zabbaleen* were despised and ignored, left to live and die on the dung-heap without attention from outside.

Sister Emmanuelle has quietly changed all this. French nun of the Order of Our Lady of Sion, graduate of the Sorbonne, teacher of Greek and Latin in Turkey, Tunisia and Egypt, she had always wanted to work with the poor. For more than thirty years she submitted to the discipline of her missionary Order, accepting her postings to schools for the daughters of privilege. But in 1963 in Alexandria, struck anew by the contrast between rich and poor, she persuaded her Superior to allow her to teach in a slum quarter. The experience increased her desire to work with the poor; the Second Vatican Council made it possible. In 1971, on the eve of her retirement, she was freed from normal discipline and permitted to remain independently in Egypt, instead of returning to the headquarters of her Order in France. Since then Sister Emmanuelle has dedicated herself to those whom, like the lepers of her original retirement ambition, nobody wished to know, a community at the very bottom of the social heap.

Or rather, on the heap; for the ragpickers live, in every sense, on the rubbish they collect. Their shacks are built on the rubbish mounds; their income and their existence derive solely from the precious cargoes trundled thither in rickety, donkey-drawn tumbrils which the men and older children drive out at dawn to the dustbins of Cairo.

It is hard to convey the wretchedness in which these communities dwell. Sister Emmanuelle's *zabbaleen* village is at Ezbet el Nakhl, near the northern Cairo suburb of Heliopolis. Here almost 2,500 people, both Muslim and Christian, live and work, give birth and die, generation upon generation. The visitor is assaulted first by the smell, the noisome odours of putrifying vegetables and acrid smoke, the stench of a settlement without a sewerage system or running water, in which humans and animals share every facility. Flies seethe in millions over every inch of terrain. One walks gingerly, fastidiously, along the garbage-strewn 'street' between ramshackle hovels, surrounded by eager children who scamper barefoot in the filth. Goats, sheep, ducks, hens, cats, dogs, the toiling donkeys, the lucrative but (in a Muslim land) illicit pigs, the pestilential rats, roam without inhibition. Women and children squat in doorways, minutely sifting the loads tipped from each tumbril, separating glass and plastic, paper and fabric, tin and wood, for later baling. The bales are sold for recycling; the middle-men of this industry control the ragpickers' incomes. Edible refuse is fed to the animals; the more delectable scraps are devoured by children. The rest is carted to a permanently smouldering pyre, or left where it lies.

Sister Emmanuelle's wood and iron shack, 9 feet by 5, opens into this squalor. Here she has lived since 1971, a ragpicker with the ragpickers, her only luxury an earth closet to which she alone keeps the key. Five days a week she used to spend on the heap, escaping only at weekends to lodge and pray with some nuns of her Order in the nearby village of Matareya. Her ambition was initially modest: to share the wretchedness of the ragpickers and do what she could, by counsel and example, to alleviate its worst extremes. She offered first aid, both medical and psychological; she started a kindergarten, adult literacy classes, sewing lessons; she gave small gifts begged from the rich of Cairo.

But after three years Sister Emmanuelle felt compelled to do more. Spurred by the death of a young ragpicker at the hands of his friends, she found in herself the courage and the will to tell the world about the *zabbaleen* and seek from it the means to build a centre not far from Ezbet el Nakhl, where the ragpickers might catch a glimpse of another kind of life and acquire some skills with which perhaps to achieve it. Her book was written before the foundations were laid. Now, the centre is almost complete. The first buildings were opened in 1980 by the wife of the President of Egypt, whose presence conferred upon the unmentionables the blessing of official recognition. Two years on, there are six imposing, grey-washed structures within an enclosure wall. A hundred and fifty ragpicker children, clean and neatly overalled, fill the kindergarten classrooms. Their mothers come to learn sewing, and to take advantage of an alternative to the annual purgatory of childbirth on the heap: a maternity hospital, plus outpatients' clinics which give particular emphasis to family planning. Young men are taught carpentry, electrical work, plumbing, metallurgy – and literacy. A social club, when finished, will wean them away from hashish and raw alcohol in the cafés of the heap. And the elderly, together with the Coptic Orthodox nuns whom Sister Emmanuelle enlisted at an early stage of the planning of the centre, will soon move into a building designed for them.

Sister Emmanuelle now spends less time in her shack. There are problems to be resolved at the centre, buildings still to be completed. She misses the simplicity of her life at Ezbet el Nakhl, but is rewarded by the knowledge that some of the new generation may now be able to break away from the ragpicking cycle to which they were previously condemned. At the age of 73, she is already looking ahead, planning to turn her attention to some of the other *zabbaleen* communities of Cairo. These are however more fortunate than their brethren at Ezbet el Nakhl a decade ago: for thanks to Sister Emmanuelle's devotion, the *zabbaleen* are no longer unmentionable, their welfare no longer a subject beneath notice. The World Bank, Oxfam, Mother Theresa's Sisters of Charity and others are working amongst them, their interest and concern a fitting tribute to all Sister Emmanuelle has achieved. Her book reveals the spirit and dedication which made it possible to do so.

British Embassy
Cairo   HILARY WEIR

To Fauzeya

Fauzeya, my sister, this book is dedicated to you because to me you represent the gospel in action. Oh, you are no theologian, Fauzeya. You don't know how to read or write and you don't use high-flown language. But as we live side by side in our little shanty-town, I know you well. A rickety bed, a chest which won't close properly, a few clothes and three or four dishes are your only possessions. You have to look after a husband who beats you whenever he has one of his fits, four children dressed in cast-off clothes (you lost four others) and about fifty pigs which don't belong to you. You feed these animals with the left-overs from the garbage collected from Cairo's luxury flats. Your life is lived between your wretched rat-infested hovel and the yard where the pigs are kept, and your bare feet sink into the muck. I watch your hands raking the ground with a piece of wood, heaping the dung into an old basket which you put on your head and empty in the narrow street outside your door. Then you set the old pump creaking as you freshen up your sweaty face, and wash your hands and dirty feet.

How do you preach the gospel to me, Fauzeya? With your transparent serenity, the smile in your eyes, the joy that radiates from you. Fine things are written about liberation theology. You actually live it: you are liberated. You are a mystery to me because, as a child, you didn't know this wretched, hard existence. You lived on the banks of the Suez Canal at Ismailia where you wanted for nothing. And what is your aim in life now? To keep your children safe, to send them to school, to provide them with a better tomorrow. As for yourself, you don't matter. You can take the knocks.

What is your secret, Fauzeya? From what living source does your serenity spring – the calm of those hands you have disowned, the suppleness of your weary body?

One evening I listened to the murmuring that I could hear through the thin board partition that separates our two homes. Your voice came to me now and then, like the responses from some low-pitched chant, answering your husband. Suddenly I realized – you were repeating the words of the gospel he was reading by the light of the little paraffin lamp. I came round to see you. You were sitting on the damp ground, breast-feeding Maryam, your latest child; your lips were slowly sounding out the words of Christ, your face shone in the lamplight. Opposite you, Guirguis, your eldest son, was doing his homework. You were at peace. Your home had 'become a light to lighten you'. God was with you. One day your children would be saved.

1. I have lived

The beginning

Twenty is an age for dreams, when life is just
beginning. I was on the channel steamer, returning
to France from England where I had gone to learn the
language.

In between visits to the Tower of London and the
British Museum, walks beside the Thames and English lessons, I had slipped in a three-day retreat of
silence before God. Now it was all settled. I would
give myself to Christ and my fellow men, and then
full steam ahead in the direction of poverty, chastity
and obedience!

'Careful . . . you're tying yourself down, my girl.'

But then my heart would be free to love. At night
in my dreams I heard the call of the unloved, the
poor, the orphans and the lepers.

It was September, the Channel looked anything
but friendly, hurling its waters on to the bridge in its
fury. Leaning on my elbows on the bulwarks, I was
smoking a cigarette in a kind of gesture to the world
that I was enjoying my freedom. A fair-haired young
man came over and started up a conversation:

'You smoke?'

'As you can see.'

It was unusual at that time and rather 'bad form'.
But as my mother had forbidden it, I took great
delight in it.

'Where are you off to like that?'

'To a convent.'

'With those eyes?'

'I shan't leave them behind on the doorstep.'

1

'Don't you enjoy adventure?'

'That's why I'm going into a convent. It's a kind of adventure.'

'I'm off to Berlin.'

'Good for you.'

'Wouldn't you like to come with me?'

'Well, no, not exactly.'

'Then it's a shame, but we won't be seeing each other again.'

I blew a puff of smoke at the grey sky. How could I get rid of this intruder? Inspiration struck: 'Would you be so kind as to find my luggage for me. I don't know where the porter put it.'

He came back triumphantly with my suitcases. We parted the best of friends and each of us set off on our own 'adventure'.

Forty-five years have gone by since then, forty-five years of marvellous adventures. Yes, marvellous. A woman, I believe, can only really blossom out and be happy in love. All along my life's path, from mission to mission, from France to Turkey, from Tunisia to Egypt, from Rome to Geneva and Brussels, the Lord has given me children and men to love. He has filled my heart with thousands of friends. I have shared their joy and their suffering, their disappointments and their loves. In order to write these lines in peace I have taken refuge beside the sea at Alexandria, the sea which saw Alexander and Pompey, Caesar and Anthony and their seductress, Cleopatra. My life seems to me to have been far more thrilling than theirs. Like the Danaides in their well forever drawing water to fill their leaking cask, these mighty conquerors scooped up empires which crumbled beneath their feet.

But starting children out on life, relieving tired hearts of their burden, grasping hold of hands about to slip into the abyss, has made me leap for joy – for the sheer joy of living; to the extent that, just think! – even if nothing grows on my grave but dandelions

2

and even if my soul eventually vanishes into thin air along with that of my cat; even then, it will have been worth the pain of turning my back on my good-looking German – and one or two others. I mean what I say. How wonderful it is to live! Which gives me an idea. On my tombstone I shall have inscribed in letters of gold: 'She lived'.

(Please note that I do not have a cat's soul. I believe steadfastly in the resurrection of the dead and the life everlasting. Amen.)

... It was 1971. I planned to fulfil my girlhood dreams and devote my last years to the service of lepers. I had arrived at the home of friends in Cairo to make inquiries. Yes, they could drive me to the leper hospital which was some distance from the city.

We were passing through an apparently interminable palm-grove.

'Stop,' a police officer pulled us up. 'This is a military zone. Your permits?'

Straight on to the police station.

'Where are you going?'

'To the leper hospital.'

The man looked at me suspiciously. 'Your papers?'

I didn't have my passport with me. He became more and more distrustful. Fortunately my companion was a charming lady who, it transpired, had all the gifts of a barrister. She pleaded so well that they let me go; but an officer was to keep an eye on me until my return.

I had to apply, it would seem, to the Minister of Health. I sent him a nicely worded request. Armed with papers, which this time were all in order, I arrived without incident. A kind doctor arranged for me to visit the meticulously clean rooms where the leper women lived in pairs. Their joy verged on delirium. A friend had come to see them. But the doctor explained to me that it would be difficult for

3

a foreigner to obtain a residence permit in a military zone. The matter would have to be dealt with directly by the Minister of Health, who would have to refer it to the Minister of Foreign Affairs, who would no doubt have to confer with the Minister of War . . . How many more ministers?! He advised me to apply to the nunciature.

So I made my way there and was received first by a young secretary, Father B, who immediately took an interest in the project. Then the nuncio arrived: 'I shall try my best to intervene, Sister, but we are in the middle of a war, there is very little chance of success. Why don't you concern yourself instead with the garbage-collectors of Cairo who live in those wretched shanty-towns?'

After some thought I decided not to inflict my insignificant person on three ministers, who were no doubt very busy. Adventure lay rather in the direction of the ragpickers.

The shanty-town

Go to the garbage dumps outside Paris or London, New York or Rio de Janeiro and you will get some idea of my Cairo shanty-town: walls made out of rusty old cans, no windows, floors of damp earth, roofs of dried palms: not a green leaf, not a flower, not a bird to be seen; but a gloomy morass of sadness in which a population of three thousand souls live and die.

How did these miserable wretches in their dirty rags fall to the bottom rung of society? Most of them came from Upper Egypt, where their meagre inheritance of a plot of ground was not enough for their needs. Illiterate, unskilled, sometimes even without papers, they are stranded in this shanty-town. How do they live? By collecting the garbage from the houses of Cairo (the road sweeping is dealt with by the local council). They leave at dawn to get into the

4

city early enough to cross the bridges, fill their small carts and be back again before the midday traffic. To prevent the theft of their wretched old nags, a child sits in the middle of the garbage while his father climbs the stairs – or vice versa!

It's an everyday sight. A skinny donkey pulling a rickety cart stops outside madam's fine apartment. A poor creature in a dirty *djellabir* rings at her door. Does she spare him a glance, either of friendship or disdain as she hands him her household rubbish? He empties it into his basket and goes off to knock opposite.

When he gets back, it's sorting time: a broken plate on one side, yesterday's newspaper on the other. Everything will be resold for a few piastres. The remains of the aubergines thrown out by madam's cook will be given to the pigs. And our children? They don't go out to play with a ball or a doll as yours do. Instead they tussle and fight over what remains of other people's garbage.

How well I remember my first visit to the ragpickers.

'*Ezayyek* – How are you?' Filthy hands were held out in greeting. We made our way carefully through the narrow streets littered with orange peel (the pigs won't eat it). Here and there an animal lay dying – a donkey, a pig, a dog or a rat. And in the middle of all that dirt were the children with their bronzed bodies and their frizzy hair. That hurt. A little boy picked up a tomato, three-quarters of which was rotten.

'No, no, don't eat it!'

His mother laughed: 'Oh, he's used to it.'

The baby in her arms was covered with flies.

All that wretchedness sucked me into it like a whirlpool. The children of men ought not to be neglected like this.

We had got as far as Labib's home: 'I'm looking for a place to live,' I told him.

'See how you like this.' He opened the door of the goats' shed for me. 'They can be put with the pigs.'

5

'It's perfect.'

There was just room for a bed, a prie-dieu, a table. What more could one want?

Labib showed me another door. 'If you like, I can empty this one for you too.'

I went inside; broken wheels and old bits of wood lay about in a sort of long passage.

'That'll make a classroom.'

It was settled. I would make a start.

In an old cart pulled by a donkey, I sat enthroned, surrounded by battered school desks and benches, a bed and a table.

We set off. Some youngsters followed us, clapping their hands and chanting: *'El 'arûse, el 'arûse'* – the bride!' Bystanders laughed uproariously. Here, when you set up house, you move your belongings to the sound of singing.

At the age of sixty-two, there I was in a wedding procession. For me, Christ was present in this shanty-town.

'Ubi tu Caius, ego Caia – Wherever you are Caius, I will be Caia,' said the young Roman wife. Who knows? Perhaps I should have dressed myself in white and invited my good-looking German and the bright young men of my youth to the wedding!

Living together

So there I was, just like a young newly-wed. Love and a thatched cottage – as a young girl I had dreamed of such things.

It was time to collect up the children. I went from door to door. A small Guirguis (George) smiled at me.

'Would you like to come and play in the mornings?'

His sister, Maryam, was older. 'And why don't you come and learn to read and sew in the afternoons?'

Frequently I was offered a glass of tea. I would settle myself down on the ground and we would talk.

These were simple people who wore their hearts on their sleeves.

Good friends had warned me: 'No one has yet ventured among those people. They're thieves and killers.'

'Nonsense! We'll see. You can come and weep over my grave.'

I think I shall escape martyrdom. What a shame! Virginity and martyrdom — as a young girl I had dreamed of that, too.

A good-natured little chap with lively eyes was following me around.

'Esmak.'

'Hey! What's your name?'

'Mohammed.'

'Well done, Mohammed. Would you like to come and play with me too?'

His mother looked at me in astonishment: 'We are Muslims.'

'Well, aren't we all children of the same God?'

'Oh, yes! *Rabbuna ouached*: the Lord is one!'

The list of names in my notebook grew longer. However would I cram all those people into the narrow classroom? But then their attendance was so irregular, I never had them all on the same day.

'Mahmoud, why didn't you come yesterday?' I would ask.

'I went with my father to collect the garbage.'

'And what about you, Nonna?'

'My mother needed me to pull the cart.'

Six-year-old Daoud preferred fighting amongst the garbage heaps. He arrived with a cut forehead. I tended to it.

'What have you been up to now?'

He was fuming with anger. 'It was Douda. But I'll smash his face in.'

'That's nice, isn't it, smashing your friend's face in.'

I waited for the face to be smashed — but it never was.

It was their feet, cut open by broken glass, that made me shudder most. They plonked them under my nose, black with dirt. 'Go and wash yourself under the pump first. I can't even see the wound.' The feet came back to me with a wide gash underneath. 'You'll catch tetanus. Go and get yourself an injection immediately. At once, today, not tomorrow!'

Soon I had become one of them. I know that some of the men are quick to pull a knife, but now if anyone looked as if they were going to touch me, there would be knives ready to defend me.

A sound Jesuit

Soon I was to be stranded alone in the middle of the shanty-town from Monday to Saturday. I felt particularly lacking in experience. I needed someone reliable to lean on, a priest capable of giving me advice. There was certainly no lack of them in the locality: Dominicans, Franciscans, Jesuits . . . I would go to the Jesuits, I knew their Superior. I thought of Pascal as I sat in the parlour, waiting for a 'good priest'.

I explained my business.

'You have all too many to choose from,' said the rector gently, and ran through a long series of names with me.

'Father X?'

'No, really he's too intellectual for me . . . I am no longer a teacher of literature, but a ragpicker. I've changed my profession.'

'Father Y?'

'Very good but too young.'

'Father Z?'

'He's only just arrived, he doesn't know the area yet. In any case, what I need above all else is a reliable priest who won't go running off next year to marry his secretary!'

'Do you know many like that?' inquired the Superior.

'No, but it has been known to happen.'

'Yes,' he remarked simply, 'but we must find out why. At the moment we test our young men for a long time. But it's a question of their getting to know attractive women so that they can test themselves properly,' he added with a laugh.

'And Father M?'

'I don't know him; is he sound?'

'Yes, he's a man who knows what he wants and where he's going. You shall meet him for yourself.'

I found myself confronted next by a man whose foundations did indeed seem to be 'sound'. We chatted and quickly reached an understanding. He was in charge of the social direction of the Jesuit college and I could see that he was moved at once by the ragpickers' story. We arranged to visit them together.

Confronted by heaps of muck and hovels made out of old cans, the priest's face took on a solemn expression: 'I shall bring our students here. It will do them good to see something other than the plush districts of Cairo.'

It was no sooner said than done. Father M arrived with a group of boys, who were at first a little hesitant, but when they saw their teacher very much at ease, sitting on the ground, talking to these people, the ice was broken. They chatted and laughed as they would among good friends. It was decided that they should all meet again and, amazingly enough, the boys resolved to hold a camp here for the first few days of their holidays. They would use the opportunity to teach our ragpickers that sport which all young people find so exciting – football.

The holidays arrived, and with them came the camp. I went round to see if they needed anything. The priest was sitting on the ground, industriously stirring macaroni in tomato sauce in an imposing cooking pot.

'Here I am, acting cook's boy, Sister. No skill is wasted – Come on, lads, who's going with Sister? – They have decided to look after the little ones in the mornings and play football with the older ones in the afternoons. And, I'm responsible for their stomachs.'

An unploughed field became the setting for pure magic. In the morning the little ones played team games; in the afternoon there was football. The camp was to end with a party in the evening.

I didn't dare to invite anyone from so-called 'polite society', because this was something of an experiment; there had never been any kind of discipline here and I anticipated complete chaos at night. To my amazement the ragpickers and the young Jesuits together had organized everything magnificently. Hurricane lamps were hanging from the palm trees. The place where each person was to sit was marked out on the ground with pegs and rope: men on this side, boys on the other. There were no women, of course, apart from me. We hadn't yet reached that stage in evolution. But that would come, later. The youngsters were supervised by two young men armed with sticks which they brandished whenever there was movement in the ranks. This 'striking' method produced an instant effect. Their behaviour was exemplary.

A succession of songs, sketches and witticisms was accompanied by outbursts of laughter from all directions. We sat there, all immersed in the same joy – children from the garbage dumps or the smart set, side by side, our hearts beating as one under God's great heaven.

After this memorable event Father M decided, together with his pupils and their new friends, that they should rent a piece of ground where they could play football: in the course of the months they developed agile knees and happy hearts. Every time

I passed by that spot I saw them leaping and running in unbounded happiness.

One fine day, unfortunately, the owner would reclaim the field; but that's another story. In the meantime, I assured myself: 'It's true, you can depend upon the Jesuits, they're sound.'

'Our sister'

After I had been sharing the life of the ragpickers for several months, I was asked:

'Tell us, Sister, where are the fruits of your harvest? Have you managed to change anything?'

I had to be honest: 'No, I have little to show for my efforts.'

'Doesn't that discourage you?'

'Sometimes, yes, but ultimately, no.' They looked at me in astonishment. I tried to understand it myself. 'Don't you see, I am here to love and to share. I have a model in Christ. What more did he do with his life?'

'And do they thank you for it?'

'Yes, but that isn't important.' I laughed. 'After all, don't you see, I haven't been crucified yet!'

Thinking about it afterwards, it seemed to me that the root of the problem must lie in the fact that, above all else, people needed to be loved – to be loved for what they are, beautiful or ugly, rich or poor, good or bad, honest or otherwise. Love them, I can, and when it comes down to it, that's what they expect of me. Shortly afterwards I was given proof of this.

Chenouda was eighteen years old. At dawn he would take his rickety cart and his subservient donkey to collect the garbage. On the day in question he walked into the garden of a convent he visited each morning, with his head held high and a new resolution in his step. A nun who was used to seeing him each day commented on the fact:

'Chenouda, good morning. How are you? How nice it is to see you looking happy this morning – like a

11

real man. For once you didn't turn up hanging your head and looking ashamed. Good for you!'

And Chenouda replied: 'Ah! that's because there's been a change where we are.' With an altered expression he added: 'We have our own sister too now. Yes, she lives with us, she is *our sister*.' His voice gave a special emphasis to the last two words and he went off, whistling.

When this simple incident was reported to me, it may seem silly to you, but tears welled in my eyes. No, I was not wasting my time if now the young men were whistling with their heads held high.

Alef, beh, teh, seh

How many of my new neighbours knew how to read and write? To my sorrow, hardly anyone. They eluded all attempts made by the government: free courses, diplomas, awards . . .

While I was struggling with the parents to get them to enrol their six-year-olds at the nearest school, I also challenged the men when I met them in the streets:

'*Yá* Morisse!'

'*Aiwa?*'

'Wouldn't you like to learn to read?'

'What use is that to me?'

'It'll make a man of you.'

He laughed, but I insisted: 'A proud man.' He looked a little thoughtful.

'Are you starting lessons?'

'Yes, in the evenings with Ostaz Ali. Will you come?'

'I'll see.'

In the end, I enrolled forty men; thirty of them started, ten kept it up. You're going to tell me that they were lazy, but don't attack my friends! I don't pull a knife, but I do know how to defend them. Tell me, dear reader, what time do you get up in the morning? I hear the carts rolling by here as early as 4 a.m. How many hours do you spend working in the sun? Not the anaemic sun found in Europe, but our sun, the real African sun. It can kill a man, especially any foolhardy European champions who dare to brave it – it will knock them out sometimes within an hour. So you must understand that these courageous ragpickers who laboriously try to sort out their *alef, beh, teh, seh* in the evenings are – well, superhuman, 'supermen' to use the modern idiom, because they have worked in the sun until three or four o'clock in the afternoon. And the others, who are not heroes (would I be one if I were in their shoes – would you?), well, they prefer to go to the café on the corner . . . what they do there is another story, a sad story.

And so when I saw them, sitting on their rickety benches, yawning as they applied themselves to their letters, I looked at them with as much love and admiration as a mother watching her son writing a thesis for his doctorate. Now and then, one of them would sigh and look up. Our eyes would meet. He would smile and start to write again: *alef, beh, teh, seh*.

'How are you?'

'Will you teach us English too?' I was asked one day by the ten who were learning their alphabet in the evenings.

'By all means, when you know how to read and write well in Arabic.'

'No,' they insisted. 'Give us at least half an hour after our Arabic lesson.'

I found a small book which gave the Arabic meanings and pronunciation and we began. It was rather difficult, but the good will was there: 'One, two, three, four, five, six,' we repeated obstinately, and finally it sank in. Then it was a question of saying a few sentences: 'How are you?' 'Very well, thank you.' They were delighted.

Whenever I encountered one of them on the other

side of the narrow street, he would rush over to me holding out his hand and crying: 'How are you?' The other ragpickers would look at their friend, full of admiration: 'Byetkallem inkelîzi – he speaks English!' My pupil would beam from ear to ear: he could speak a foreign language.

Great was the joy whenever by chance I met their little carts in the streets of Cairo. They would call out a cheery greeting while I gave them a friendly wave. Sometimes even – 'Whoa!' – they would stop the donkey to get down and shake me by the hand. As they did so they would glance proudly to left and right: no, not everybody despised them.

How little it takes to help a man recover his dignity: a handshake, three words in English. 'How are you?' and the all too commonplace answer, 'Very well, thank you', becomes concrete and real. Suddenly the man really does feel, 'very well, thank you'.

Building? No problem!

It was becoming impossible to breathe in the crowded classroom. We needed to expand, which presented a somewhat thorny problem because the pigs also needed vital space.

After a long palaver and vain attempts to find another place, I was advised to 'build an extension on the side facing the street'. That was all very well, but with the pile of muck in the middle, how were the carts going to get past? Careful calculations were made: it could work. Our amenable neighbours proved to be in agreement.

It only remained for us to start on the house. That wasn't difficult. As a matter of fact, with us the problem of materials is simplified: a hole is dug, water is poured into it, straw is mixed in and slap-bang wallop! the wall is put up with two bare hands. So why are there these old cans everywhere? Because the rag-pickers are a far-seeing people who need to be able to carry their homes on their donkeys. One fine day the neighbouring peasants will have had enough of this pig farming and may well come to drive them a little further away. (The laws of the Koran forbid the eating of pork.) That being the case, off they will go – out will come the nails, the walls will be salvaged and they will leave just as they came. In Europe they call it prefabrication. The Cairo ragpickers invented it a long time ago.

The roof isn't complicated either: the stems of reeds covered with old palm leaves do the trick. But what happens when winter comes? It's simple enough, they stretch a sort of oil cloth over the top and keep it in position with stones. As Rousseau once said, it was civilization that caused all the problems.

The joinery was not yet complete, but we could move in our benches and set to work. Suddenly there was a dreadful noise, the whole building trembled, and threatened to collapse. Terrified, my little girls began to run yelling towards the as yet doorless gap. I followed them. A lorry that comes from time to time to collect the dung and take it away for the peasants to use as manure, had run into the wall. Had it been going any faster, we would have been underneath the rubble – or more accurately underneath the reeds and the palms. There's an additional advantage to a house of this kind – when it falls down, it doesn't kill you.

For all that, I was slightly concerned. Next time there would be nothing we could do but sit down on bits of wall and dried reeds and lament our lot. But then Labib's father had an enormous stone brought over and calmly placed it at the foot of the wall. If the lorry ran into that, the driver would notice it and be more careful another time. Everything here has a simple solution.

God is love

All that was missing now from our new palace was the door and the windows. The joiner arrived and we came to an agreement. The walls were colour-washed in pale pink – it was beginning to look almost elegant. String was stretched along the walls, with clothes pegs so that we could hang up our children's masterpieces. They drew, they painted, they stitched and they proudly hung up their own handiwork. Clay models of donkeys and pigs reclined with a genial air on a plank beneath a vase of wild flowers.

The door was long overdue but it did arrive in the end. It was made out of a conglomerate, because wood is expensive here. Zachareyya showed me his masterpiece. He had carved out a cross and a crescent and fitted the one into the other. He had also made up some wooden letters which he had carefully positioned underneath: *Allâh mahabba* – God is Love. Zachareyya watched me out of the corner of his eye. I was so pleased that I wanted to fling my arms round his neck and kiss him; but such outbursts have to be curbed – I didn't want a public scandal.

This kind, simple-hearted Muslim had understood of his own accord why I am here – simply to remind our Christian and Muslim ragpickers that God is Love. Yes, God loves them, because I am only a poor creature fashioned from the same clay as they, but in me lives that Breath of Love which makes me give my life voluntarily to change theirs. I know the One who brought this fire into the world, and it is to its burning Source that I go each day to rekindle the small flame which possesses me.

My attempts to help them are often doomed to failure, but if my passing amongst them has left them with the single reminder that 'God is Love', I will not have been useless to them. A divine seed will have been planted amidst the filth of the garbage, and in the midst of death, life will blossom anew.

A Letter

In 1972 I wrote in a Christmas letter:
My dear friends,

Christmas is coming, which provides me with the opportunity to pass on greetings from our friends the ragpickers. They cannot send you a pretty greetings card, only the joy which shines in their eyes at the thought of the distant friends about whom I have told them and who take an interest in them.

Trying to give joy to others – isn't that what we are all doing, especially during the Christmas period? I am amazed when I see how my hands are filled with good things to enable them to spread joy. First there was the little passage which is now in the process of changing into a spacious, light room. In the morning the little ones will come to play there: dolls of all sizes, educational games, coloured blocks with Arabic letters and numbers on them, beads to thread, Plasticine, coloured crayons, pots of paint and even a teddy bear await them. Thanks to an excellent session with a kindergarten teacher I was able to learn about these things and to obtain the necessary materials. They will help these intellectually underdeveloped children to enter a world other than that of garbage and pigs, and get them ready for school.

In the afternoon it is the girls' turn to have the room and be taught the alphabet and needlework. The patterns for some large dolls are all ready. Each of them is going to make one for herself or for her little sisters, together with an outfit for it. Then they will be taught the rudiments of dressmaking and how to use the sewing machine, something which they all dream of. It only remains for them to be instructed in child care and first aid. *Bishweishe, bishweishe* – all in good time. A small contribution from Caritas-Egypt helped me to get all that under way.

The greatest consolation of the year, however, is the sight of thirty or so youngsters going happily to

17

school with their small cloth bags containing exercise books and textbooks under their arms. It is a sight never before seen among the ragpickers but now the parents are very proud: 'Do you know, Soraya already knows how to write her name,' her mother told me with emotion. What a struggle it was to induce her to register her daughter! But on the day when she finally set out for the school with the necessary papers in her hand, what a marvellous sight it was to see Soraya trotting behind her with a shining face. Her little heart sensed dimly that she was taking her first step towards a new life.

It is these little ones who will come in the evening to run through their lessons again under the supervision of a teacher: a large paraffin lamp, desks and benches take the place of the small candle and the damp earth of their hovels. Afterwards they will vacate the room for the men who also want to learn to read and write. They are able to do so thanks to lessons given by Ostaz Ali, a young student at the Muslim university of Azhar.

Evening is the best time for family visits. We all sit on the ground round the candle and these simple people tell me about their difficult life with all its suffering and its sorrow. 'Oh, if only we had listened to what you said about Maryam, she would have been at school instead of falling off the cart and being run over by a car!' Silence ensues. Her mother weeps silently on my shoulder. 'We've got to leave here, but that means we have to find work elsewhere.'

At Luiz' house, we chat: 'How many cigarettes do you get through in a day, Luiz?'

'Two packets,' he replies, but his young wife interrupts him 'No, three packets.'

'Isn't that too many?'

'You're right, but our life is so difficult you know – morning, noon and night spent amongst the filth. I smoke to take my mind off it.'

If I am with Christians we share the gospel together.

Often I learn from them and sometimes when I hear them speak so profoundly about the message of Christ, I can only repeat his words: 'I thank thee, O Father, Lord of heaven and earth, because thou hast hid these things from the wise and prudent, and hast revealed them unto babes.' They possess that treasure – the wisdom of God. The inspiring title of Bouchaud's book, *The Poor Preached the Gospel to Me*, has become a reality for me. One day Om Magdi had only ten piastres when she went to visit an orphan girl, 'She is worse off than I am,' she said to herself, and gave the girl everything she had. That day she didn't eat. Isn't that literally living the gospel?

What a wonderful lesson in courage I had, too, from a young woman doctor who comes to look at the women and children once a week after her work at the hospital. One day when the Khamsin was blowing and it was suffocatingly hot I wasn't expecting her, but suddenly she appeared and had to sit down before she fainted. 'But, Mimi, why on earth did you come in this boiling sun?' I protested.

'I have always wanted to repay the nuns who brought me up for all the goodness they showed me. Isn't this the best way of doing it – by putting what they taught me into practice?' was her reply.

As for the Jesuit students, each week they cement their friendship begun with the youngsters during their holidays, by coming to coach them at sport. This week they are getting ready for a major event. They are going to have a football match in the famous field that we rent. Having a sports ground like that is an innovation which, I believe, is very important. These young people are starting their education with the opportunity to train in Egypt's most highly rated sport and, what is more, they can do so in the company of those who belong to what is known as 'polite' society. The financial problem remains a painful one, however, because each month we have to find the necessary money to rent the field.

This life has given me the opportunity to experience something inconceivable to anyone who has not been through it. Living day and night as one with the most deprived brings with it a ray of that perfect joy which Francis of Assisi experienced to the full. That hot summer's evening, when even the water in the pump gave out and I had to go to bed in a tiny little room next door to the pigs, with rats for my companions, something extraordinary happened. My heart, ever insatiable like the Danaides in their old well, seemed suddenly to be freed from its burden of constantly renewed desires. All at once it was flooded with a marvellous indefinable joy. The fountain of living water promised by Christ gushed out in torrents.

Everyone finds the path to liberation in their own way: a mother confided to me that she had found it in the middle of a labyrinth of difficulties overcome by love; a businessman in two of his workmen who had suddenly become like brothers to him. May the Christmas star continue to guide us towards those marvellous occasions when we are flooded by that unutterable joy, which springs from God — that of sharing with our fellow men, our brothers.

Wild flowers

'Today, children, we are going out for a walk to pick flowers.'

With cries of frenzied joy, my flock of sparrows rushed in confusion towards the swinging door. They all wanted to go out at the same time and the mud wall was about to collapse.

Eshak, the monitor, gave me a reproachful look, then sprang into action: a cuff here, a cuff there. 'Romani, stop that! Hoda, if you carry on, you won't come with us. Daoud and Guirguis, don't fight. Everyone sit down in your places.' He yelled to make himself heard. Crestfallen, our youngsters sat down again on their little benches.

Eshak was right. I should have told them first that we would only take the good children on the walk. We made them cross their arms to avoid them punching their neighbours and they went out a bench at a time . . . the door survived undamaged.

Now they ran along the paths, a few paces apart – it was better that way. Otherwise they fought to pick the same flower. Each one clutched a fistful delightedly to his heart.

We sat down in a circle on the ground, flowers in hand.

'Aren't the flowers lovely, children?'

'Na'am, yâ ableti.' 'Oh yes! big sister,' they yelled with conviction.

'Who wanted there to be beautiful flowers on the earth?'

'Rabbuna, our Lord,' they cried at the top of their voices.

I tried to calm them down a little – we looked in turn at the trees, the fields, the water which gurgled along the little canal and their small eyes were filled with beauty. We thanked God for so many good things: 'Nashkorak yâ Rab.' It was decided that we should put the flowers in a tin in our hut to brighten it up a little.

We set off again, with full hearts. The flowers were crushed between small fingers – they were so unused to handling delicate things. Poor little souls, they had never been away from their hovels, never picked a flower, never gazed at nature. Raise yourself from one beauty to the next, said Socrates, until you reach the supreme Beauty. Children climb very quickly!

Thalassa! Thalassa! The Sea!

The rains had begun. It took courage for our girls to come to their lessons through the narrow streets which were ankle-deep in mud. In the end, eight of

21

them stuck it out. I decided to reward them. We would go to see the Nile.

We set off, singing our way across fields already dried by the sun which had by this time reappeared. On to the train we hopped, then into a tram. Unnerved by such an unusual outing, they huddled around me like fledglings in a finely balanced nest.

At last we drew near to the Nile. As soon as we set foot on the platform, they could contain themselves no longer: with arms outstretched, they began to run, shouting aloud, 'El bahr, el bahr, the sea, the sea!' Suddenly I thought of Xenophon's ten thousand Greeks. Spanning a gap of more than two thousand years, this enormous sheet of water provoked the same ecstasy of frenzied joy now as it did then – el bahr! el bahr! took up the echo of Thalassa! Thalassa! With their eyes popping out of their heads with admiration and astonishment, they leaned on a ledge and fell silent.

Poor little girls, who knew nothing but squalor and pigs. They would soon reach the age of puberty at twelve or thirteen and would no longer be allowed out, even to come and see me. Then they would be married off and all they would have for baggage would be the little that I had had time to teach them.

Samia Mohamed, a charming little girl quivering like mercury, came over to me. Her big dark eyes looked up, brimming over with joy. Then she seized my hand and kissed it effusively. The other seven didn't want to be left out and all of them tried to hug me at once. My veil was about to slip into the Nile but I caught it just in time and hand in hand my little girls, suddenly quiet again, set off once more with light hearts. The pigs and the garbage mattered little now; they too had seen the Nile.

Aida

Her name was Aida – a name from grand opera. She was fourteen years old with enormous dark eyes which lit up a laughing face. Like a desert gazelle she came bounding up, and went off again like a flicker of lightning, singing as she went.

'Aida, come and learn to read and sew a little.'

She laughed, shrugging her shoulders: 'What good would that do me?' She was engaged, and already the man to whom she would soon belong didn't want her to go out of her hut.

A woman went by with a basket of mandarins on her head.

'Bi-kâm – How much?'

'Five piastres a kilo.'

'You've got to be dreaming. Five piastres! That's far too expensive. Here's three and a half.'

A heated discussion ensued. Aida would not give in. She threw down three and a half piastres and wanted to grab the mandarins. Voices were raised. They were on the verge of fighting.

'Look, Aida, she can sell at whatever price she wants. Either buy or don't buy, but leave her alone.'

She went off with a bound of fury. What could life hold in store for this unmanageable filly, this little uncontrolled soul?

'You know Aida?'

'What about her?'

'She poured paraffin over her head and set fire to herself!'

They told me the pitiful story. She had broken her ear-rings. What was she to do? She gave them to a man who was passing through to repair. He came back – her ears tingled with joy – but he was claiming his money. Aida ran to her mother.

'What, he wants fifty piastres? Are you mad?' In her fury, her old mother poured a torrent of abuse over her daughter.

Beside herself, Aida went back into the hovel, seized the can of paraffin and emptied it over her head. Quickly, a match!... Her hand trembling convulsively, she seized it... Tragically, her clothes and her whole body went up in flames. She died three days later in excruciating pain.

No one had taught Aida, the little gazelle, how to control her impulses. Her father died shortly afterwards; her old mother remained alone, a picture of grief, clutching a pair of ear-rings in her hand. So it is that we live and die – for baubles!

The outing

Would you, my reader, like to do a quick calculation? With the days you have off for weekends, the Christmas and Easter breaks and the summer holidays, how many days of leisure do you have in a year? Possibly not far off a hundred, or perhaps even more, if you include Saturdays?

Last year I tried to give just one day's outing to the men who came to learn their alphabet in the evenings. The Jesuits had promised me a coach. We could go to the Pyramids, stopping off here and there along the route.

The students had all assembled for their class. My young friend, Ostaz Ali, the future sheikh of Azhar, had written some exercises in addition and subtraction on the blackboard. 'Now, lads, would you like us to go and visit the Pyramids next week? If we leave early in the morning, we can go to the zoo, and anywhere else you would like to stop. – Yes, we could visit St Theresa of Choubra,' suggested Ostaz Ali. (That mysterious little saint is much loved here by Muslims and Christians alike.)

'You could take us to visit your university and the Azhar Mosque too,' I added in my turn.

The first murmur of enthusiasm was followed by

a kind of depression: 'Mush mumkin, – It's impossible,' they said.

'Why? We shall have the coach free of charge.'

'We never have a day off.'

'What, never, not even a Sunday or a Friday?'

'Never. People can go without food for a day but not pigs. They might die.'

And if they didn't go and collect the garbage what were they to give the animals?

'So in the entire year, you don't have one single day's holiday?'

'Yes, for the festival of Mar Guirguis (St George) we take two days off and buy food for the animals. That's all.'

Silence ensued. Inside I was seething. What slavery those pigs brought with them! The drivers of the carts depended on the swineherds, their masters, and even the actual owners of the animals were subjected to the same regime of forced labour.

At last I suggested, 'It's summer, we can come back at ten o'clock at night. What time can you leave in the afternoon?'

'We're not back before three or four o'clock.'

'Can't you make it before then? At two?'

'Kwayyes – All right, we'll try.'

The coach was waiting in the road. I went to collect the men. At two o'clock, Ostaz was there with Chaaban, at two-thirty Ibrahim arrived but by three o'clock no one else had turned up yet. We would have to leave, for it was a long way to the Pyramids. We gathered up some little boys who were hanging about – they were delighted at such a marvellous windfall – and off we went. On the way we met our friends, still a long way from home. They gave us a long, sad look. It was heartbreaking. If it hadn't been for the small boys shouting and singing, the excursion would have been a dismal one.

We arrived at the Pyramids. Their dark mass seemed as immovable to me as the destiny of our ragpickers. I felt as if I were crushed with them beneath those enormous blocks.

But where were Hamdi and Fahmy? All around me, noses were pointing upwards. I pointed mine in the same direction and stifled a cry. Two shapes were fearlessly scaling the blocks of stone. They reached the tip of the pyramid safely but then their descent seemed to last a lifetime. What did that old Cheops want with a 138-metre high tomb anyway!

At last Hamdi and Fahmy landed beside us with one final victorious leap.

Lord, now can I help our ragpickers to rise above their destiny with a similar leap?

The students

The Jesuit students were still visiting us regularly. Rami would call by to pick up the ball and then off they went to the sports ground. One Sunday, one of those torrential downpours, which are fortunately rare in Cairo, was beating down on the city. For several days water fell from the sky in cascades. The paths were ankle deep in slimy mud so I waited for everything to dry out before returning from the convent to my shanty-town. I telephoned Rami.

'Sister, you weren't there yesterday.'

'No, of course not, with these impossible paths.'

'Not as impossible as all that, Sister. I got through.'

'What about the mud?'

'Oh, I survivied it. The children were expecting me, you know.'

How plucky these young people are! They are always one step ahead along the way.

Reda is another faithful one. The youngsters particularly appreciate his true and unequivocal friendship and the brotherly hand he offers them. They like to have long talks with him. Sensing that he understands them, they discuss things with him man to man.

26

The holidays were drawing near when Reda arrived.

'I have an invitation to spend a month or two in France, you know, Sister.'

'Aren't you lucky? When are you flying?'

'I'm not going.'

I was thunderstruck.

'No, I prefer to stay with my friends here.'

How many young people dream of travelling abroad? Others prefer the ragpickers.

Unfortunately Reda's father fell seriously ill. A Lebanese, he wanted to go back to his own country for treatment. Reda had to accompany him. His father felt better and returned to Cairo but soon he was called to be with God. Our ragpickers were grief-stricken at the news. Some of them called on their friend to tell him how much they shared in his sorrow. In one of the reception rooms in his apartment I saw them sitting completely at ease among other 'distinguished' guests – it was a rare and reassuring sight.

Ezzat spent his holidays going from one settlement to the next trying to nurture those little ones who never had the opportunity to play enough – or to eat enough. For me, too, he was one of the most effective sources of encouragement. I wanted to take advantage of the days that remained before the schools started again, to set those children to work who still couldn't read after attending school for two or three years. With classes of possibly fifty or sixty children, what could teachers do with those of our little ones who were slow to understand?

'Ezzat, will you come and help me for the remaining three weeks?'

'Willingly,' was the reply.

The university was organizing a trip to Alexandria. For this young man, who had spent his holidays in the service of others, it must have been very tempting

— sea, fresh air, friends and outings. Too late I discovered that he had given it all up.

'But you could have done with some relaxation too!'

'Sister, you know how attached I am to you and the ragpickers.'

Of that, I had proof enough. Every morning I watched him come and coach each small pupil through his lesson with infinite patience. We did some general revision and, triumph of all triumphs, our children began to read. Ezzat did not bathe his sturdy body in the waters at Alexandria, but his spirit was possessed of singular joy. He had rescued some little ragpickers from ignorance.

Sameh spent all his Sunday afternoons with us. He too, became a great friend of our youngsters. He took them for ball practice and wanted to form a scout troop. 'They're changing gradually,' he told me in confidence. 'They're developing a team spirit.'

Young people like that are terrific.

A ministry

It was absolutely vital that I found a doctor to visit the ragpickers regularly. All I could provide them with was daily first aid. But who was going to agree to come to such a wretched place which was inaccessible by car?

I had heard talk of a remarkably dedicated and unselfish doctor. I went to see him in his clinic in the fashionable district of Heliopolis and I had no sooner explained the situation than he agreed.

'All right, Sister, I will come once a week. What day would suit you best? I am committed to the service of the poor ... When I was young,' he confided, 'I was torn between the priesthood and being a doctor. One of my teachers said to me, "Antoine, you've got what it takes to become an excellent doctor and save a good many people." So I decided to make medicine my ministry. Part of my practice is among the poor, and as for the rich – if you only knew for how many melodramas I try to provide the cure!'

So there he was, wading through the filth in the narrow streets. He was horrified.

'But, Sister, you could catch just about any illness here!'

'Come now, doctor, we have all been vaccinated – more or less!'

Rats as big as cats ran between our legs. Flies buzzed in our ears. He looked at me, obviously preoccupied. I laughed: 'Yes, doctor, I can see what you're thinking. Soon I shall catch bubonic plague, exanthemic typhoid and green cholera, which could send me straight to my grave. But if I do, then you'll save me, doctor, won't you?'

He entered the tiny room which I had carefully had whitewashed. Suddenly he breathed again. 'It's clean in here.'

'Yes, of course, doctor, and as the fleas were multiplying rapidly, I had tiles put down and we swill it out every day.'

Slightly reassured, he began to examine the sick. I admired the way in which he treated each one with respect. He lingered over some of the more serious cases. 'We must keep an eye on them,' he insisted. One woman was incapable of getting up, so he crossed the shanty-town to her hovel. 'I shall send her some special medicine,' he promised.

Under a leaden sun, he set out to find his car. His step was light as he went off, perspiring but happy. He had just relieved a multitude of ills. Yes, Doctor K, for you medicine is a ministry.

He was pregnant!

A fair proportion of our ragpickers come from Upper Egypt and they have kept its primitive customs, particularly as far as women are concerned. Hus-

29

bands won't always allow their wives to come and
see the doctor. Now that they know I am present
during the examination most of them are reassured
– but not all of them.

Om Anwwar was suffering from dizzy spells. She
was waiting her turn but seemed worried to me. 'Get
me through quickly,' she pleaded. She came in, then
suddenly I saw her turn pale. Her husband was
looking at her through the skylight, his face rigid
with anger. 'He didn't want me to see the doctor,' she
explained.

'Wait, I'll talk to him. – Abdel Wahab, why are you
angry?'

'There's nothing wrong with my wife. It's all play-
acting. I had forbidden her to go out.'

'Come on, Abdel Wahab, I've noticed what a good
father you are, how concerned you are when Anwar
has the slightest thing wrong with him. So why can't
you be as good to your wife? Promise me not to beat
her?'

She went out, hardly reassured. He grabbed her by
the arm and they crossed the street together. Did he
refrain from beating her? I daren't be too sure.

The bold Fathy arrived next, and recounted how
for the past month he had been suffering from
dizziness and sickness. The doctor listened attentively to his embarrassed explanations. Suddenly he
said with a laugh, 'You're sick all right . . . you're
pregnant, my friend! Is your wife pregnant?'

'Yes,' he replied, uneasily.

'Right, try and bring her to see me and, in the
meantime, give her this for her stomach.'

Fathy went off well pleased and no doubt firmly
resolved not to have his wife looked at. The doctor
and I burst out laughing. 'In Upper Egypt', he told
me, 'it's common. The men come to be examined and
give their wives' symptoms. Even the most inexperienced young doctor doesn't take long to recognize
that they have problems – they're pregnant.'

2. Darkness and light

A trick of the shadows

Rather like the great fairs of the Middle Ages, fairs here are the happiest occasions for a get-together. My little girls explained to me that they would not come to lessons on the following day because they were going to the 'Fair of the Blessed Virgin'. 'You ought to come, *Ableti*, all the Christians come, and the Muslims too.'

It was settled. I joined a group, and we climbed on to a cart. About thirty of us piled in and sat with legs crossed, or, as I did, with them dangling over the side. It wasn't all that uncomfortable. The people sang, laughed and clapped their hands. They called out to carts coming the other way. Here was the joy which overflows from the good people of God. We jumped down, the women took out two piastres from the knots in their handkerchiefs and, with their children on their shoulders or hooked to their skirts, they started walking. Soon we were lost in the crowds.

Ritual had it that we should start with a visit to the sanctuary of the Virgin, *El 'Adhra*. We took small steps forward, marked time, then moved forward again. Everyone was shouting and singing. At last, there we were in the church. Men armed with sticks were instilling a little order into the throng by beating those who didn't want to keep moving. But the beaten and the beaters were laughing together. Nevertheless there were some who remained stoically in position despite the blows. They were waiting for a play of sunlight shining through the trees, to form a vague silhouette. Then everyone would shriek for joy: 'El 'Adhra, El 'Adhra, the Virgin, the Virgin.' Those who could, stroked the wall to make more certain of a baraka, a blessing.

Poor simple people, didn't they see that it was only a trick of the shadows? But those shadows were enough to give them faith. I don't know why, but I couldn't help thinking of Plato's cave where the men in chains, too, could see only the shadows of those who passed behind them. What do we see of others but a dim shadow – which often seems to be quite enough for us?

The faith of these good people transforms everything for them. I looked at their faces. They were exultant because they had at least seen something like a shadow cast by heaven. To my calculating brain and cold heart the whole thing seemed a ridiculous masquerade.

To me, yes, but for these simple souls the finger of God was still writing on the wall. Aren't other, more authentic, symbols offered to us each day? But then how does one learn to decipher them with such exultant joy?

Cross

The fair offered amusement to all for twopence – shaggy heads to knock down, swings to soar you to the sky, red cones to be worn as hats, pink sugar dolls, the chance to try your luck here, coca-cola to drink there.

There was a man holding a poker with a burning tip. He dipped it in a blackish liquid and made people's skin sizzle. 'He's a tattooist. I am going to have a cross tattooed on my children's arms,' Malaka explained to me.

The verse from the Song of Solomon resounded in my ears, 'Set me as a seal upon thine arm.' I held out my wrist. The man smiled at me – a foreign woman having herself tattooed! The burning tip sank in; there was a searing pain, a smell of scorching and the cross flowed on to my skin. There was the outline marked indelibly on my wrist, but would I know how to carry it in my heart: the cross, the suffering of the world?

Malaka was talking to her eldest. He was eight years old. He could understand what it meant to be tattooed. He would suffer for a few moments but then he would bear the sign of the cross unto death. 'Fahmy, are you proud of being a Christian?' The child looked at his mother – quite the young man – then resolutely held out his wrist. He gritted his teeth and didn't flinch. Magdi's five years, however, didn't rise to quite the same lofty heights. He yelled and struggled while his brother kept a determined hold on his wrist. Then it was over. He could see the black cross on his little pink arm. His tears dried and he waved his arm about proudly.

'Salib', 'cross', is a name borne proudly here by many Christians – which brings me to the story of Salib, a tram conductor and the father of nine children. Life was not easy for him. I received a letter from rich friends of mine in France: 'We would like to adopt two little children from a poor family.' Sure in advance what the answer would be, I went nevertheless to Salib's house.

He called his wife and began to laugh. 'You want us to give up two of our children? – Never!' He bent down to five-year-old Selma: 'Would you like to go to a beautiful country, Selma, where you'll have a pretty dress and lots of sweets?'

Selma flung herself at her father and buried herself in his arms. 'Lâ, lâ, No! no!'

Salib turned to me: 'Each of us must carry his own cross. I will never cast off the burden of my children, and besides, they are a great joy to me.'

I have never seen a family so full of laughter and song as this little nest full of fledglings. There was always one of them sitting on their father's knee. It didn't matter how much bread and onions they ate . . . whenever Salib came home, without fail, one of the little ones would fling himself round his neck. Is it really for an easy life that children hunger first and foremost?

Salib, too, had had himself tattooed with the sign of the cross.

Danger in the maize

The number of small children coming to learn to read and sew had increased that summer and the heat of all those young bodies squeezed into the building, even with its extension, produced an unbearably stuffy atmosphere. I found a large hall adjoining the church in the neighbouring village. There was a small yard to play in. I could have the use of it during the holiday months. So we moved in!

The girls were delighted and every day they brought new friends with them. We had never before reached the fifty mark as we did now. Reading, writing, arithmetic and needlework, catechism for the Christians, morality for the Muslims followed one after the other, interspersed with ball games. Everything was for the best in the best possible world, as Candide would say!

Suddenly the number of girls began to drop. One afternoon there was only a handful left. What on earth was going on?

I questioned them. Why weren't the others coming? They looked at each other and announced in unison: 'Durra! durra! The maize, the maize!' Suddenly frightened, one of them exclaimed: 'I shan't be coming any more.' – 'Nor me,' added another.

I didn't understand.

'The maize, *Ableti*, they are killing people in the maize. They've got two of our children.'

I managed to get to the bottom of it all. None of the

children had actually disappeared, but the peasants had put the word about to stop them pilfering as they went through. Murder in the maize? Yes, it does happen, particularly in Upper Egypt where honour must be avenged with blood. If a girl is courted with too much familiarity, if someone is insulted or sustains a theft, they wait until the maize is two or three metres high. Then they hire a killer for between five and ten pounds. He lies in ambush among the stalks, kills off his appointed victim and slips calmly away. Justice has been done.

It was my turn to go through the maize. Suddenly there were hurried steps behind me. Was it the killer? I felt so isolated on the narrow path between two hedges towering above my head. The ragpickers, at least, were all my friends. Yes, but then anybody could be coming through here. I must face it out. I turned round sharply with a pounding heart.

The man quickened his pace towards me and called out, 'Don't you have a cross you could give me? Look.' He showed me a cross tattooed on his wrist. I showed him mine.

'My sister's daughter is sick.'

'Listen, I don't have anything on me at the moment but I'll give you one another time.'

He beamed at me from ear to ear. New found friends, we carried on walking together in between the high stalks.

Once the maize had been cut down and the danger had passed, our little girls returned.

The film show

How could I revive the dormant faith in these people who only ever set foot inside a church on the day of the Fair of the Blessed Virgin? Holy Week was drawing near. What about showing them a film on the Passion and the Resurrection?

The hall next to the church was a spacious one. I

35

went in search of the priest in charge and we soon came to an agreement. He gave me two hundred tickets and he would hand out the others in his parish. 'The number of tickets doesn't really matter,' he said, 'they'll never all turn up.'

It was a much bigger success than I had dared to hope for. My children sold the tickets between them and faithfully brought me the two piastres for each one. I was only left with about ten and I was quite right in thinking that I ought to be there at six.

Evening was drawing in. The room filled up with good parishioners who had some idea of punctuality. I was worried. My flock had hardly begun to arrive and the hall was already full. That was it – there was no more room. The priest had the doors closed and gave directions to start.

There was the sound of fists banging on the door. 'Open up, open up! We've got tickets.'

From inside came the shouted response, 'You're too late. There's no more room. You were supposed to be here at six o'clock, it's now seven.'

'What! They had paid two piastres and it was a film about the Messiah and they weren't to be allowed in? They'd soon see about that!

The banging was redoubled and the door began to give way. Ostaz G summoned his young men to the rescue and together they set their backs to the splintering door. At last with one final blow from the shoulder, our hefty men from Said came in shouting. The priest frantically grabbed a whip and tried to drive them back – to no avail. They pressed forward in closed ranks, squashing the parishioners, who by this time were terrified, ever further together. Then, much moved, they punctuated the film with their exclamations. When Christ appeared, bearing his cross, they clenched their fists. Oh, if only they had been there! – as Clovis said of his Franks.

When it came to the Resurrection they went into a frenzy of applause, creating an indescribable hubbub.

The parishioners, increasingly squashed by the last late-comers, wondered anxiously if they would ever get out of the place alive.

At last the film was over. Beaming with joy our ragpickers took their leave, each one coming to shake me enthusiastically by the hand.

Then, brave souls that they were, they said goodbye to the priest with his whip hanging motionless at his side. The parishioners, freed at last, went out in their turn, giving me black looks. No doubt they are godly people, but, when it comes down to it, who looked on Christ most lovingly?

'Adhra Maryam – the Virgin Mary

Fauzeya was resting wearily on a bed covered with flies, with a little bundle of pink flesh beside her.

'Give me a nice name for my little girl.'

'That's for you to choose, Fauzeya. To my mind the name which has the most beautiful ring to it is that of the Virgin Mary, El 'Adhra Maryam.'

Her pale face lit up: 'Yes, yes, we shall call her Maryam,' and she cradled the little parcel in her arms delightedly.

The cult of the Virgin Mary has remained strong in the East. Even the Muslims fast in her honour. But there are sometimes scuffles with the Protestants. Taki, for example, is fervently orthodox. The other day, he was waiting for the doctor in the little square outside my shanty when suddenly I heard shrill cries coming from that direction. I rushed out. Taki, as red as a rooster, with his eyes bulging out of his head, was about to attack the Protestant Beghit. Each was yelling his side of the argument in the other's face, without listening at all, of course. The two roosters quietened down a little on my arrival and Taki, sure of my approval, remarked to me: 'Did you hear that, he doesn't believe that the Blessed Virgin appeared at Zeytoun!'

I tried to calm him down by speaking gently to him, 'Taki, doesn't Beghit have the right to think what he likes?'

Then I turned to the other man: 'Beghit, go on through to the doctor now if you'd like to.' He vanished, happy with the turn of events.

'So you think he's right?'

'Now look here, Taki, do you think you'll persuade him otherwise with your fists? When you've laid him out on the ground, he'll start invoking El 'Adhra Maryam, I suppose?'

'What about you, don't you go to Zeytoun to pray to the Virgin Mary?' he inquired without answering my question.

'Of course I do, it's an important place.'

'So you believe in the appearances, then.'

'Taki, I know that many Christians and even some Muslims claim to have seen her. As far as I'm concerned, I join in their hymns and that's enough. El 'Adhra Maryam is wherever she is invoked.'

Suddenly he remembered that he was not well and joined the queue for the doctor.

The gallant Taki was prepared to strangle a man for the sake of the Virgin Mary. Without his ever realizing it, he had become a disciple of Ignatius Loyola in the early days of his conversion. I ought to tell him the story of the mule. Ignatius was travelling along with a Moor. After a heated discussion on the subject of the Virgin Mary, the latter whipped up his animal and made off into the distance. The knight's heart was pounding beneath his breast-plate. How dare he insult his Lady? 'Holy Mary, in your name I shall sacrifice him.' With his hand on his sword, he urged his mule forward. (Taki, you will tremble for joy at this story, but wait and see what comes next, my friend.) They arrived at a crossroads and the Moor turned right. Ignatius was not after all altogether convinced that he should split his skull. 'Better submit myself to God's judgement. If my mule gallops to the right, then I shall slay him outright.' He let go of the reins, and the mule turned left.

Taki will no doubt tell me: 'The animal was a peacemaker!'

Happiness for five pounds

Some French tourists, passing through, had left me some local money that they wouldn't be using any more. It came to five Egyptian pounds, about five pounds sterling. When I got back, I found Fauzeya gloomy and quiet. I hardly recognized her. The children were crying and squabbling. What was going on? Her husband was going through a depression and didn't want to work any more. He spent his days at the café, drinking and gambling away the few piastres they had. 'Tell Guirguis to go and get him,' I said. The little boy ran off and soon his father appeared.

'What's happened to you, my friend?'

His expression was sad and distant. 'I am too tired, I can't work.'

We chatted and he relaxed a little.

'Listen, I noticed that quinine did you some good last time. Would you like me to get you a bottle?'

'Oh, yes!'

'All right, come and get it tomorrow evening, Saturday. I shall be with the other sisters at the sisters' house. But first, do make the effort to go to work in the morning, otherwise you know you'll risk losing your job.'

'Of course.'

It was six o'clock in the evening when he appeared, exhausted. 'See, I'm on the way back from the factory. I've seen the works doctor. He told me: "You should have a little radio and when you get home tired you should relax and listen to some music. That'll calm you down better than going to the café, and what's more, it won't cost you anything." It's all very well for the doctor to talk but I don't have a radio.'

'How much do they cost?'

'Three or four pounds.'

'Well, you're in luck! Yesterday some tourists left me a little money. Let's go and buy you your radio.' He could give me the money back sometime, if ever he was able.

We stood outside a shop and there was a transistor for three pounds seventy-five. We went in and bought it together with a bottle of quinine to put father back on his feet, a packet of cocoa for mother who was fasting on water, and some grapes and peaches for the children. The radio was playing a happy tune. The furrows on the man's brow had relaxed, joy shone in his eyes which had come alive again and he laughed with relief. 'Ah! I shall be able to work and I won't need to go and listen to the café radio any more.' His family life was restored to normality, saved by five pounds!

They sing

I still have a lot to learn about our ragpicker friends, particularly about a certain approach to life which manages to nip tragedy in the bud. Where we are, instead of sacrificing Iphigenia, Agamemnon would have tucked his helmet under his arm and left the camp under cover of night. We have no heroes, and when it comes to military service a fair number of them will discover that they have lost their papers, a fact which provides them with automatic exemption. I have not seen a single one come back from the war parading his wounds. They are conscientious objectors without even knowing it.

The woman, who with loud screams, is beaten to a pulp on Monday, has often forgotten all about it by Tuesday, and is heard singing cheerfully behind her rusty tin walls. There are no complexes here. When he saw the huge supplies of nerve tonics that had been donated to us, the doctor burst out laughing. 'You want to send those to the wealthy districts, Sister. They use them a lot there.'

It is this resilience which saves them and enables at least some of them to bounce back in tragic circumstances which would completely flatten other people.

The only reality they have to contend with is the event of the moment – that's their only philosophy from infancy to adulthood. Their capacity to bounce back never ceases to amaze me.

Samia had long been looking forward to an outing to the zoo which we had been planning. On the morning we were due to go, she arrived in tears, 'Mummy doesn't want me to come. Come and talk to her.'

I went.

'I can't let her go. Don't you see? She'll have to look after the pigs and my little boy. I'm not well today.'

Gently I stroked Samia's damp cheek: 'How will your mother manage without you, *yá habebti* (sweetheart). Won't you stay and help her?'

Samia looked up at her mother with eyes still misty with tears. 'I'll stay with you, mummy – You'll take me with you next time, won't you, *Ableti*?'

She hugged me and ran off happily to look after the pigs, humming *'Yá mama, yá Helwa'* – O mother, o pretty one.

It is one of the mysteries of the human heart that those who have the most always want more: a financial giant can't get to sleep at night, while those who have the least come to terms with their lot – our shoemakers and ragpickers – sing.

The elephant

A major event was in progress – we were off to the zoo. Little feet ran happily along the narrow path which overhung the ditch and the gurgling canal water below. How joyously they skipped through the fields to the waiting coach. (Once again it had been loaned to us by the Jesuits: it's good of them because coaches are difficult to buy and you can't get spares for old bangers!)

We were in the city now, and the children waved delightedly at our friends with their carts as we went past. For once they weren't being hauled slowly about by some old donkey, but travelling along at top speed in a real bus.

We arrived and everyone got out.

I divided up my flock with draconian directions. 'You must stay with your group of five, and the person in charge of it must keep counting you. Those who don't do as they are told and keep having to be called to order will not come with us next time. You might get lost. Only the other day, back where we live, a mother lost her little girl. She was shouting and crying through the alleyways: and her little girl must have shouted and cried too, when she turned round and couldn't find her mother. What would they do alone here, far away from home and lost in this enormous park?' Suitably scared, the children promised to be good, and we set out.

Our first stop was at the ostriches: 'What are they called? What do they eat?' We moved on, and the pink flamingoes perched on their stilts watched coolly as we passed. Suddenly there was a roar. My little girls huddled together.

'Don't be frightened. It's a lion but he's in a cage.'

Trembling with fear they drew nearer. He opened a mouth, so enormous it made you shiver – and yawned! They laughed with relief. Another, stretched out with his head between his paws, was sleeping – or daydreaming. Lions weren't all that bad after all.

'No, but be careful. Last year a careless keeper had his arm torn off. Come along.'

At the reptile house, the inmates were all behind panes of glass. Quite unafraid, the children pushed their way to the front, calling out whenever one of the creatures moved or coiled itself up. But where was the crocodile? Under water probably. They kept on calling it, *'Yâ Timsah yâ Timsah'* – but there was no sign of life. He was having a swim.

Ever anxious, I spent my time counting and re-counting my lambs, five at a time. They were all there so we went to have a look at the monkeys.

This time there was a long pause for reflection.

'They look just like people, don't they?' I heard one of them say to another.

'They must be the ones who were turned into monkeys for being wicked.'

How about that? Our young ragpickers had become philosophers and quite spontaneously come up with the idea of the transmigration of souls!

The parrots were calling to us. One of them cried out, *'Yâ Hassan, yâ Hassan!'* every time his keeper whispered in his ear. The children had to be prised away: they kept turning back to look at this strange talking bird.

What on earth was that enormous animal over there? *'El Fîl, El Fîl'* – an elephant! This time, with no regard for either groups or obedience, they took off as fast as their legs would carry them. The elephant's trunk rose and came down, grabbed a cucumber and gulped it down so rapidly that it provoked a torrent of laughter from the children. I had literally to tear them away from its vindictive trunk. They cast a very indifferent eye over a polar bear pacing round in circles. Pooh! a bear is only a little thing but the good Lord must have made the elephant!

And with their eyes full of that gigantic vision, they left triumphantly. They would certainly have something to tell their families!

The slave

A woman came to the dispensary for treatment. Her eyes had disappeared into a face so swollen, she looked like a bulldog.

'Is this your first visit?' I asked her, 'I haven't seen you before. Where do you live?'

'Don't you recognize me?' she answered hoarsely, 'I'm Hanem.'

'Hanem, it can't be! Is it really you? What on earth has happened? What's wrong with you?'

'My husband beat me.'

'Why, what did you do?'

'Nothing, he's just like that!'

I sat her down and examined her poor bloated face and her poor pain-racked body. He must have flung her on the ground and kicked her.

'Listen, you're going to have to go to hospital for treatment and have a few days' rest to sort you out.'

'It's no use, he'll never let me.'

'What time does he get back with his cart?'

'Four o'clock.'

'Right, I'll go and see him.'

She shivered: 'No, no, don't tell him I've spoken to you. He'll beat me up again.'

'Don't worry!'

At four o'clock I went to see him. He was sitting propped up against the leaky tin walls of his hovel.

'Well, Mikhail, how are you?'

'Not bad.'

'Listen, I just bumped into your wife. She's got a very strange-looking face.'

'She fell off the roof.'

'You're joking! When people fall off roofs, they

44

may break something, but they don't get heads like that.'

'All right, if you really want the truth, I beat her.'

'Why, what did she do?'

He stood up, with renewed fury, his eyes bulging out of his head. Wait until he found her he would beat her again!

I squatted on the ground beside him. 'Sit down, Mikhail. Calm yourself. Just tell me, quietly, what she's done.'

'All right, listen. Yesterday I left, at four o'clock in the morning, as usual.'

'Yes, I sometimes hear your cart go past.'

'She went back to bed and fell asleep again.'

'There's nothing unusual about that. All the women do the same. What then?'

'What then? She left the door open with the key in the padlock. A thief came along, *kanet nayma*, she was asleep. He went in, *kanet nayma*, she carried on sleeping. He stole the radio, *kanet nayma*, and she carried on sleeping. He stole my *djellabir*, *kanet nayma*, she carried on sleeping. He stole the padlock and the key, *kanet nayma*, *nayma*, *nayma*.' With each *nayma* his voice went up a note. He wasn't far from shattering his vocal cords.

With a look of thunder, his lips tightly pursed, he added with a hoarse cry: 'She made me lose thirty pounds, nearly thirty guineas, *Yesmayi kwayess* do you hear?'

'Yes, thirty pounds is a lot of money,' I said sadly.

'It's a lot of money,' he repeated after me, pleased that I had understood.

'Now that you've beaten her, have you got all that money back?' I went on softly. He looked at me, slightly bewildered, and made no reply. 'And now that you've reduced her to such a state, you'll have to send her to hospital and that'll mean even more expense for you,' I added quietly.

'It's not worth her going.'

45

'But if she isn't properly treated, she might not get better and then who'll look after your pigs?'

The argument struck home. I left him looking shaken. All the same he sent his wife, or rather his slave, to hospital. As in the days of the ancient Romans, all she was entitled to was bread, work and the stick.

The flies

The education of women remains one of my main concerns. It's one area in which I have achieved very little worth mentioning. When I walk through the alleyways of the shanty-towns and see them, dirty and in rags, breast-feeding rickety babies covered in pustules, in the middle of the refuse, my courage fails me in the face of my own powerlessness to extricate them from it all.

Swarms of flies settle in the corners of their eyes and cover the faces of their babies, lying on beds which are also black with flies. I made some little white veils and put one over Fathy's half-naked body. That evening I went back happy in the thought that he would have been saved from the flies. A disgusting black rag was trailing on the ground. I recognized the little veil which only that morning had been immaculate.

These women are brutalized by too many pregnancies in rapid succession. They give birth, then one or two months later there they are, pregnant again. A doctor whose advice I sought suggested I set up a government birth control centre, but it isn't as simple as that. The women would be scandalized at the idea of my running a centre of that kind, and anyway, I might find myself confronted by methods that I couldn't condone, like sterilization.

All I asked for was a nurse, who was a specialist in the field. She appeared and, as she didn't know these parts, I had to go with her on her first rounds. I kept out of the way but I heard a group of women around her laughing and mocking her. God sent babies! Why did she want to go and interfere? And it was I, a nun of all people, who had brought them a black sheep like that!

The nurse refused to come again. She didn't like them making fun of her. So what next? I would have to start first with the very simplest things, like general hygiene.

I went in search of a government department which, I had been told, specialized in films of that kind. I actually found it and came to an agreement with the director. The first film he would send me was on the subject of flies. Our experience with the parish priest and his worthy parishioners had demonstrated conclusively that it would be better to stay on home ground. The sports field might do, but we had no electricity laid on. No matter; a lorry with a battery could transport the equipment, the director suggested. I particularly wanted the women to be there. 'Tell their husbands that the government made this film specifically for the women,' he advised.

I always make a point of asking them for a minimal contribution so I made up some tickets for one piastre. Highly delighted the men offered me their piastre: 'Mind you don't come without your wife,' I told them. 'The government has sent this film for her.' One man looked at me aghast. His wife going out, and in the evening of all things!

'Don't worry, we're using the football ground as a cinema – women on the right, men on the left. I shall see to it myself.'

The man hesitated. His wife insisted: 'See, the government has ordered us to go.'

'I couldn't care less about the government, you're not going.'

Hm, this could turn nasty! 'Listen, Fatma, if he doesn't want you to come, let it drop this time. When he sees other women at the cinema, he'll let you come next time.'

That evening there were several hundred men on the left, and, despite everything, about fifty women on the right. We sat on the ground, separated by a carefully extended piece of rope. An animated fly appeared on the screen and buzzed about all over the place, hotly pursued by a little goblin. The audience roared with laughter. The fly was just about to land on the meat when, wham! – the goblin knocked it senseless. What an odd story, they thought.

Next a nice clean housewife appeared and threw the waste into a pretty bin carefully covered with a lid. There was renewed hilarity!

I had also begged a colour film from the Japanese cultural adviser. It showed a fairyland of multi-coloured butterflies fluttering among pink cherry trees. The audience were at the very peak of enchant-ment and those sitting next to me thanked me enthusiastically. I was pleased to have broadened their horizons for a few hours, but the story of the stunned fly and the carefully closed bin was as far removed from reality for them as the Japanese fairy-land!

Several hundred had come to the show but some-how there wasn't quite such a large number of piastres rattling about in the wallet. I discovered that some of the youngsters had been playing at counter-feiters and forging tickets which they had sold.

The balance-sheet for this first attempt was not very positive. But then – when all was said and done, they had had a good time and, what is more, miracle of all miracles, there had been women present!

Mother's Day

I decided to make a big occasion of Mother's Day; in trying to teach the value of women it was easiest to start with mothers.

For the past month the little ones in the morning and the older girls in the afternoon, had been singing the song:

> Yâ mama, yâ helwa
> O mother, o pretty one.

In the kindergarten they had designed and coloured some little cardboard boxes for sweetmeats: in the afternoon the girls were embroidering handkerchiefs (if not very finely). One of them came to me. 'Will you draw a cross for me, in the middle of the handkerchief?' I complied. Thrilled with this idea all the other Christian girls nearly suffocated me by milling round brandishing their handkerchiefs.

'Salib! Salib! – a cross!'

'Be patient. One at a time. God has only given me one pair of hands. I shall have to ask him for another couple of pairs.' They laughed, envisaging me as a Hindu deity with four or six arms.

Not to be left out, the little Muslims came running up: 'Will you draw me Mahomet's window?' Hm! I'm not very well up on the subject. Never mind, let's have a go. I drew a rectangle with a grating. They were ecstatic – but what would their mothers say?

One morning in the kindergarten, I called for silence: 'Pay attention. Listen carefully, all of you. Are you given a piastre every now and then to buy sweets?'

A chorus of well-fed voices answered me: 'Na'am, yes.'

'This week you are all going to keep your piastres to buy sweets for your mothers.'

The chorus fell suddenly silent.

'You all love your mothers, don't you?'

'Na'am,' the chorus replied with conviction.

'Do you love them more than you love sweets?'

The chorus faltered again but I refused to be daunted.

'It's a wonderful thing when children love their

49

mothers more than sweets! Now let's see, I'm sure I
have lots of good children like that in front of me!'

A hand shot up: '*Ana, ana!* Me, me!'

'See, I was sure that Romani loved her mother
more than sweets. Well done Fawzi, you too. And
Samia, too, well done!' One by one small hands
bestirred themselves. 'That's excellent, you can all
bring me your piastres and we'll give your mothers
a pretty sweetmeat box full of sweets.' One piastre
would only buy two sweets, but I have some good
friends overseas and I have never found my purse
empty. My urchins gleefully piled in the sweets,
knowing full well – the little scamps – that they
would have a good share of them.

The older girls were going to make a cake. They
too brought me their piastres but, in their case, there
were no objections. Since it was Lent and we were
fasting, we couldn't use any animal produce: no
butter, no eggs, no milk. The young monitress had a
recipe for a Lenten cake and with great enthusiasm
we set about making it. The ingredients, for the
benefit of any one interested, were as follows (of
course we greatly increased the quantities):

> One cup of oil (225 g)
> Two cups of sugar (500 g)
> Two cups of orange juice (1 kg of oranges)
> Three cups of flour (500 g)
> One packet of baking powder

They all peeled and squeezed the oranges and, with
carefully washed hands, they blended the mixture.
Téréza lit the oven she used for baking bread. The
cake was borne over to it in procession and they all
sat down on the ground, round the oven and chat-
tered until it was baked. Marvellous! They devoured
it with their eyes. It might well be meant for their
mothers tomorrow – but the children would have
some too!

The great day arrived. The boys were impeccable

in their clean *djellabirs* and, with ribbons in their hair, each of the girls looked prettier than the next. The mothers arrived, much moved. It was the first time in their lives that anyone had fêted them in any way. The children sang, gave recitations and wrote a few words on the blackboard. Their mothers' admiration was all the more intense for the fact that these mysterious signs were mere hieroglyphics to them.

It was time for the presents. Everyone brought out either their box or their handkerchief filled with sweets. They kissed their mothers: *'Eid Saîd!* Happy Mother's Day!' and promised to be good.

At last the famous cake appeared in triumph. It was carefully cut into pieces and everyone had a good helping. The mothers all left beaming, clutching a sweetmeat box or a handkerchief in one hand and a child in the other: each double set of similar eyes sparkled with the same joy.

In the evening the men arrived to learn their alphabet.

'Why all the streamers?'

'Because it's Mother's Day, of course! What did you do for yours today?'

They looked at me in astonishment.

'People are fêting their mothers throughout the country today so why aren't you?'

I used the moment to say to them: 'Do you know what really upsets me? How much you beat your wives!'

This time I had lost them completely. Ibrahim spoke up for the others. 'But our women don't understand anything! What else can we do but beat some sense into their heads?'

'You could explain things to them, reason with them.'

'Reason with women!' They laughed: *'Mafish mukh,* they've got no brains,'

'So, I have no brains.'

That embarrassed them. Ibrahim spoke again: 'You have, but you're not a woman.'

Ostaz Ali, their young teacher had come in for his lesson. Silence reigned. I was left pondering. So what sex am I? Not masculine or feminine – the only thing left is neuter!

The doll

I had been given a nice fat banknote by some friends. How could I use it in the best interests of our little ragpickers? What if I bought them a doll? I have so many times seen the face of some little prospective mother light up as she cradled one in her arms. I could even make it some clothes which the sewing class could use as a pattern.

So I found myself in a large store, gazing at a delightful talking doll, and imagining Victor Hugo's Cosette suddenly clasping this marvellous present in her arms. What pleasure it would give my dear little urchins, too. They had never played with a doll in their lives. I dressed her in the style of the girls in Upper Egypt, in a long dress made out of a light cotton fabric, and carried her through the narrow streets: she provoked a passionate interest. The news spread from shanty-town to shanty-town; men, women and children all came running to see a talking doll. We named her Sabrina and I gave my solemn promise that all the children who attended classes regularly would be able to play with her.

Sabrina became like a living person, everyone's friend.

'Look how clean and well groomed Sabrina is. Wouldn't you like to be as pretty as she is?' And quickly out came the little comb so that its owner could look like Sabrina. Romani, a little fellow of seven, gave her a resounding kiss on both cheeks, exclaiming: 'I'm going to marry Sabrina!' Then each child in turn cradled her in ecstasy. The poor little thing talked so much, that her voice recording became quite hoarse. Sabrina was ill, the children announced compassionately. We would have to take her to the doctor. 'Ssh, let her sleep, don't make a noise.' They talked in whispers and walked about on tiptoe: Sabrina had worked her first miracle!

Money isn't everything

Eshak, the young monitor, is a charming boy. He very quickly became a friend of the ragpickers. The little ones in the kindergarten, by some miracle, don't move an inch when he's giving them a lesson. He does, however, have one serious fault: he has no idea of punctuality. In vain I have reminded him repeatedly: 'Eshak, we start lessons at 9 o'clock.' I might as well have saved my breath. He turns up at 9.30, 10 o'clock, 10.30. Only on Mondays is he on time. Why? Very simply because when I come out of mass I call on him and wake him up, and we go on to the shantytown together.

Perhaps, after all, I thought, we should be patient. He was waiting for the government to arrange a posting for him and he did have a family to support. When he was four years old his father had died while his mother was pregnant. The child was born healthy but, at the age of twelve, he was suddenly attacked by a mysterious illness. Seeing him climbing the stairs on all fours, his mother shouted at him angrily: 'For the last time, Ibrahim, walk properly!' — 'But, Mother, my legs won't hold me upright,' came the reply.

Half the small house was sold to pay for hospital fees — to no avail, he never walked again. Eshak adores his brother and takes him for rides in his little cart. Every now and then he takes him to a cinema some distance away and gets home late at night on his last legs. On the following day, quite naturally, he arrives late, but how can one hold it against him?

In January his mother went to Upper Egypt to collect a small inheritance. 'I'll take the housekeeping money for the journey. The neighbour owes us a few pounds, so you'll have enough until the end of the month.' She went away with an easy mind. But the honest neighbour suddenly vanished and Eshak and Ibrahim found themselves in a tight spot. I noticed our young monitor arrive looking sad and worried. Under a barrage of questions, he ended up telling me the truth.

'Well, Eshak, why didn't you tell me about your difficulties? Can't I take your mother's place while she's away? I'm going to lend you what you need. It's very easy. You can give it back to me later.' Eshak went away, happy to be able to give his brother a decent meal.

In March, the international exhibition was due to open. Because of his knowledge of French, Eshak had been given a well-paid job there for a month in the previous year.

'The exhibition is coming up,' I reminded him, 'I shall try to arrange things without you.'

'Not on your life. I'm not leaving you.'

'Come on, Eshak, be reasonable. You'll earn ten pounds, that's a fair sum. You'll be able to buy some lovely presents for Ibrahim like you did last year.'

'But it's Ibrahim who doesn't want me to go. "Eshak," he said to me. "Money isn't everything. Sister helped us out a few months ago. You can't let her down." '

In vain I insisted. He kept on repeating: 'Money isn't everything, Sister, money isn't everything!' And, believe it or not, he was a little more punctual that month!

'She's my mother'

Eshak had long dreamed of going to France – so Father M had found him a job as a holiday organizer, because he has a way with children. All he had to pay for was his travel. We agreed to put a little of his money on one side each month. I would keep it for him so that it didn't go up in smoke – cigarette smoke. The only thing he lived for now was this adventure, so he was feverishly sorting out his documents.

One day he arrived looking drawn and as yellow as a lemon. 'I wanted to throw myself in the Nile,' he said, with a voice that seemed to come from beyond the grave.

'– ? – '

'But as I bent over the water to jump in, it looked a bit too muddy to me. So I abandoned the idea.'

'You were right . . . But why all the melodrama?'

'Everything was rolling along nicely,' he said with a lump in his throat, 'immigration formalities, passport, etc. I was happy, so happy. Then suddenly, just as I was getting my ticket, the man says to me, "First you must pay a deposit of fifty pounds into the bank. Without that – no ticket!" It hit me like a bomb. The whole idea was crumbling around me! So I went down to the Nile like a sleepwalker.'

He seemed so desperate that I couldn't help feeling sorry for him, 'Calm down and let's see. The bank will give you the fifty pounds back when you return?'

'Oh, yes, of course, but I'll never find that amount in the first place.'

'Instead of rushing to the river, you should have rushed here.'

He looked up with a glimmer of hope in his dark eyes.

'Now let's try and find some people to help you out. If we can find several of them we could well end up with a loan of fifty pounds for you.'

The suggestion met with a sigh of relief, and a smile which began to shine like a rainbow through a stormcloud.

Our objective was just about in sight when all of a sudden Eshak turned up with a yellow skin and tousled hair. What had happened to this hypersensitive young man now? He smoked away without a word, then suddenly he banged on the table with his fist. 'I shall go.'

'You will go, Eshak, you will, but bear in mind how fragile the table is. It doesn't want to get in your way.'

'My mother won't let me go.'

'Why?'

'Because some order, supposedly from the government, arrived saying that all those who graduated in my year would start work this summer.'

'So what happens if you're in France?'

'My mother says I shall lose my job.'

'That has to be true, Eshak.'

'No, it hasn't, and in any case I don't care, I want to go. Everything is ready. I can do without her permission!'

He was so exasperated that it seemed wise not to say anything in reply.

'Yes, I shall go to France, or Libya, or else I shall throw myself under a train.' He lit up a second cigarette: 'But I shan't stay here and be bored to death.'

'You were looking forward so much to this government post. Why let it slip away from you now?' He shrugged his shoulders, stubbed out his cigarette and walked away.

A short time afterwards his mother arrived in a very agitated state. 'Have you seen Eshak? He didn't come back last night!'

'Yes, he's just left.'

She sighed with relief. 'The boy's mad! He wants to lose his job! What will become of us? He's the

56

only source of support for Ibrahim and me.' She choked back her tears.

'Be patient, Eshak has a good heart. He'll listen to reason in the end.'

Next day he turned up, the eternal cigarette in his mouth: 'I've decided to stay.'

'Well done, my friend.'

'Yes, I said to myself: "Your mother has remained a widow, she has brought you up all by herself since you were four years old." ' He stubbed out his fag-end in the ashtray. 'Yes, she's my mother, I can't break her heart.'

One month later, Eshak took up his post as secretary at the university. That evening he came to see me, as proud as Punch. 'It's my job to register the students and they have already told me that I may be able to work overtime. One day I shall buy Ibrahim a television.'

'Is your mother pleased?'

'Oh yes, I want her to be happy, she's my mother!' And he beamed so broadly I could see all his teeth, yellow with tobacco.

3. Breaking down the barriers

Learning to love one another

From the moment I arrived among the ragpickers I was struck by the divisions, sometimes very hostile, which existed between the religious groups. In the early days I used to take one of the little girls with me to explain to people what I was going to do for their children. She would tug at my skirt: 'No, don't go there. There's no point, there isn't anybody there.'

'What, can't you see those children over there?' I would exclaim, and carried on.

In the end I realized what was happening. If the child acting as my guide was a Christian, she would try to stop me visiting the Muslims, and naturally, the same would apply in reverse if a little Muslim was accompanying me.

One important task ahead would be to try to bring them closer together: I must make the most of every opportunity.

I took the Christians on their own for lessons in religious knowledge. While the little Muslims sat outside and listened to an exciting story with a moral, I subjected Maryam, who was especially bigoted and who had assured me several times that only Christians were good, to a series of questions:

'Is Fatma a nice girl?'

'Oh yes.'

'She doesn't say unpleasant things to people or hit them?'

'No.'

'Is Fatma a Muslim?'

'Yes.'

'So do you think all Muslims are wicked?'

She didn't answer.

We were coming up to Holy Week so I explained to them that Jesus loved the whole of mankind and died to save us all. They agreed so I added a syllogism: 'Are Muslims part of mankind?'

'Certainly.'

'Does Jesus love all of mankind?'

'Yes.'

'So Jesus loves Muslims too.'

This time I sensed that they were disturbed.

'And if Jesus loves them, shouldn't we love them too?'

In the end they let themselves be convinced. On the following day I had some little crosses ready to give them, and to avoid complete chaos, I called them in one at a time.

'Tell me who you love?'

'I love sweets, mummy, Mar Guirguis (St George), God and daddy.'

'Is that all?'

'No, I love my little sister too, and Sabrina.'

'Is that all?'

The little girl could see that I was waiting for her to answer before I gave her her cross. She gave it some intense thought. 'I love Muslims too,' she exclaimed suddenly.

'Well done.'

She went away triumphant, prize in hand.

The other girls – the little rascals – had been listening at the door. 'I love Muslims, sweets, mummy, El 'Adhra (the Blessed Virgin), God and beans,' recited the next one to arrive.

They each received a cross and went away happy. I had to laugh at my all too primitive methods of persuasion, but it does seem to me that, more than anything else, their seeing that I love them all as my very dear

children is beginning to draw them together. Isn't it as
they each receive the same love from their mother that
brothers and sisters learn to love each other?

The missionaries

One evening I went to the Coptic-Catholic church for
mass and bumped into the priest. 'Ah! the sister from
the garbage people. I have a preacher this evening but
wouldn't you like to speak too? The church will be
full.'

'My Arabic isn't very classical!'

'What does that matter? Talk about your people. It
will be good for us.'

So I found myself standing in front of the inconos-
tasis with my back to the twelve apostles: that augured
well. I set about explaining (with occasional stam-
mers, but they seemed to understand) that in the eyes
of God a garbage collector was as important as the
president of a Republic (I didn't dare say 'sometimes
even more important', it would look as if I wanted to
overthrow the State). Yet sometimes people flung him
their garbage without so much as looking at him and
that was quite simply that! Unfortunately, too, like
most people who left their home village, these people
had also given up practising their religion. They were
now like sheep without a shepherd.

After the service, some people gathered round me in
the square outside the church. 'We're ready to go and
see them, Sister. We'll read the gospel to them and sing
terâtels' – these are canticles which Egyptian Christians sing at the top of their voices with an enthusiasm
which defies comparison.

'Fine, but they belong to the Orthodox Church,
they're Baba Chenouda's lambs. Don't catholicize
them.'

'Of course not!'

We fixed a day and a time and off we went! How
good it was to be going out to meet kindred spirits even

if they did have to paddle through muddy paths to get there!

The ragpickers vied with each other for the pleasure of entertaining the new missionaries. They shooed the pigs from their yard, hung a paraffin lamp on a nail and crowded tightly around their visitors who sat on an old up-turned oil drum with their feet on the damp earth. They listened in silence, they sang at the top of their voices and repeated the prayers as prompted. The man who had organized the visit was radiant. A breath of God had breathed on these people in their darkness! I went from one group to the next: 'Ah! tonight we are really receiving a *baraka*,' the ragpickers told me with beaming faces.

Those who had come to bring a little love and joy went away with the smell of the pig farm clinging to their shoes and yet, as if borne on wings, they sped happily on their way.

How beautiful are the feet of them that preach the gospel of peace!

Baba Chenouda

I hold the present Coptic-Orthodox patriarch in as much veneration as Athenagoras, who had welcomed me with such warm cordiality some years before when I had taken my pupils to meet him in Istanbul. He too was a man of God. After much serious learning and theological study at the university he became a brilliant teacher who attracted hundreds of young people. Then suddenly, he disappeared. Where did he go? To Europe or America, attracted like so many other great brains by the dollar and its delights? No, that wasn't his style.

Rumour has it that he shut himself away in the desert in the strictest of Orthodox monasteries. For years he stayed there, fasting, praying and meditating, but such a light could not be allowed to remain hidden indefinitely under a bushel. One day an envoy from Patriarch

Kyrillos came across the sands and banged on the door of the monastery. The order was quite categorical. He must leave his mud-walled cell, his mat and his life of silence, and return to the hubbub of the city. He was made a bishop despite himself, but whenever he could, he would escape to the monastery to be with God, 'He who is beyond everything' as Gregory of Nazianzus would say.

Kyrillos' strength had begun to fail him by the time I brought my pupils from Alexandria, where I was teaching at the time, to Cairo.

At his residence we were met by a smiling bishop. The girls rushed forward to kiss his hand. 'It's Amba Chenouda,' they whispered to me.

'We would like to see Baba Kyrillos,' I said.

'He's not receiving many people at the moment.' As I drew near I took an instant liking to this kind bishop. 'All right, I'll try and telephone, just to keep you happy.'

That was my first contact with the future patriarch; he managed to get us an audience. Baba Kyrillos was visibly tired but happy to lay hands on all those young heads who were so pleased to see him. He also blessed me, at some length.

Three months later this faithful servant was called home to his master. The millions of Copts waited in suspense: who would be their new patriarch? The voters were made up of more lay representatives than clergy. Three names must be selected and then, as in the days of the early Church, offered to the Holy Spirit. In the middle of the solemn liturgy of the mass, in the enormous basilica of Morkoseya, the large number of assembled people appealed to the Lord: 'Kyrie eleison-ya Rab irham.'

Three names written in large letters were shown to the congregation and placed in a casket in the middle of the altar. One of the three was that of bishop Amba Chenouda.

A five-year-old child toddled up to the altar. The

celebrant bent down, opened the casket and offered it
to him. As the child's chubby little hand grasped one
of the bits of paper the congregation held its breath, for
the name chosen by this little innocent would be the
Lord's anointed. Suddenly the roof resounded with
the name of 'Chenouda'. The people were beside themselves with joy. Their future pope was a holy man.

The day of the consecration had arrived. I had
received an invitation for nine o'clock but I had been
forewarned by a well-informed friend: 'Be there at
seven or you'll find it impossible to get in.' An enormous crowd was already spilling over outside the
doors, held back by hundreds of police officers in
ceremonial uniform. Fortunately, being not too fat, I
managed to find a place in the throng and by some
miracle a sudden movement landed me outside the
outer door. Phew! There I was, safe and sound in the
courtyard. That was one obstacle successfully overcome. Pushed to the right, jostled to the left, squeezed
from the front, pummelled from behind, I pressed on
undaunted.

Climbing the steps one at a time was another delicate
operation, but I managed it by a series of fits and starts.
There was only one last remaining obstacle – the door
of the church which was closed and blocked by four
men and a corporal; it was already full up inside. After
all they couldn't risk suffocating the newly elected
patriarch in mid-ceremony! I noticed, however, that
when a fat monk in front of me brandished his card,
the police, no doubt impressed by the fullness of his
habit, extricated him from the crowd *manu militari*
and magicked him away inside.

I stood on tiptoe, raising my veil above the heads of
the crowd and brandishing my card. The effect was
unmistakable; the four men tried to reach me to extricate me in my turn. The ideal solution would have
been to throw me a rope and hoist me over the billow-
ing tide, but one can't think of everything. However,
the corporal, a herculean figure doubtless specially

chosen that day for his formidable biceps, suddenly charged at the sea of chests. The crowd was yelling. I didn't want to be responsible for people dying on the church steps! At last he grabbed me as if I were some kind of prey and flung me through a chink in the door which opened just for an instant. Fortunately I landed on my feet with all my limbs intact.

The men were on the left and the women on the right, as is usual in Orthodox churches, no doubt to avoid distractions. I slipped in behind the long black veils of the Orthodox nuns who told me they had been there since 5 a.m. These daughters of God, set apart by the circumstances of their rigorous confinement, couldn't risk being jostled by so extraordinary a throng. The crowd had become noisy and restless but then, suddenly, absolute silence reigned as the imposing liturgy of the Coptic mass began, interspersed with prayers asking God to grant strength to the newly elected pope. The time had come for the tiara to be placed upon his head and I watched Baba Chenouda. He was deep in prayer. With his eyes closed, this monk was visibly placing his whole being in the hands of God.

His shoulders drooped slightly, he lowered his head and a shadow passed over his solemn face which bore the expression of a man suddenly weighed down by too heavy a burden. The tiara was on his head. In the eyes of God and men he had become responsible for millions of Copts. The congregation rose, trembling with emotion. Cheers of joy thundered out, women wept silently and, as Baba Chenouda looked at his people, his eyes assumed a new expression: veiled by a shadow of sadness, they seemed to burn with immeasurable love.

It was all over and the nave gradually emptied itself but part of the crowd remained clustered round me. I asked why. 'He'll be leaving by this door. Whatever happens, we want to kiss his hand.' We waited. There was a movement from the direction of the chancel.

Baba Chenouda was coming, preceded by an escort of fine strong men, but who could stop a crowd bent on kissing their patriarch? The guard was scattered, a prelate who came to the defence of his pope was knocked over and with cries of triumph, in an indescribable mass, the crowd pushed, squeezed and squashed their new pope from all sides. He was bound to be suffocated! The earth remained powerless to save him, heaven was the only resort. Help, all you Coptic saints in paradise, come to the rescue of Chenouda III!

All at once a squad, made very much of flesh and blood, surged through a door which burst open. Force was the best policy – with blows to left and right, the rescuers forced open a gangway and, in the twinkling of an eye, they had spirited the victim away behind the door which ground shut behind them. Nothing daunted, the crowd directed its onslaught against the wood. The unfortunate door had had too much to put up with. With a shudder it gave way and the people rushed through in triumphant pursuit of their pope. Too late! He had evaporated and vanished into thin air. These good-hearted people burst out laughing. They had been the victims of a clever trick, but all was not lost. They would kiss his hand at the very next opportunity.

It reminded me of Paul VI's visit to Jerusalem. He too was nearly suffocated by the crowd. The Oriental likes to touch: 'If I may but touch the hem of his garment,' said the woman in the Gospel.

The death of children

Mimi, the young doctor, was examining a succession of sick people with her usual dexterity. I had been feeling feverish and ill all day and it didn't take Mimi long to notice. She examined me and gave me decisive orders: 'You can't stay here tonight, Sister. It's not on. I can't tell you what's wrong with you yet, but you're coming back with me to your sisters at Matareya.' I was reluctant to leave my friends, but my head was burning and I wouldn't be much use to them.

In the end it turned out to be paratyphoid that tied me to my bed. My temperature wouldn't go down and the sisters called the doctor again. Just as he arrived a friend, who was also a doctor, came up the stairs, and much to my embarrassment, they both found themselves at my bedside.

So much professional care soon put me back on my feet and I made straight for my shanty-town. The news that awaited me struck me to the quick. Six-year-old Aouni had died, and two days later so had his four-year-old brother. Aouni used to come to the kindergarten every morning in the very pink of health. A well-built, strong and chubby child, he was the epitome of life – perhaps even a little too full of life, because he would never stay in his place, and when he disturbed the others too much, I used to have to say to him: 'Go home to your mother for a while, Aouni, and come back when you can behave.' Fortunately, he lived close by.

So what devastating illness had taken him, together with his little brother? They had had measles. Nearly all of us catch measles when we are children but we don't die! But how could these children be properly looked after in that dismal hovel? Their two sisters, who came to see me in the afternoon, told me through their tears how in the end Aouni had been taken to the doctor; he died on the way. The other little one had been left to die where he was.

And at that very time, by some fateful irony, I had had two doctors at my bedside. Who should really have received attention? Those who were starting out on life, or one who was nearing the end of it? I have known life with its joys and its sorrows. My life has been thrilling because it has itself engendered life. I am ready to go home to the Father. But who will resurrect those little bones, now buried beneath the ground? Which of the three of us should have died?

66

How could I resign myself to accepting the suffering and death of children? Rebellion welled up inside me. Wasn't God Lord over life and death? What was the answer? The meaningless world of Camus or Sartre? Blowing your brains out with a bullet, as one father did, beside himself with grief?

A highly intelligent woman who was at one time my Superior used to say: 'When your head is swimming, turn to the Bible. It's a book for the learned and the ignorant alike.'

Job, as he sat on his dung heap, said to the grave: 'You are my father'; to the worms he said, 'You are my mother and my sister'; and to the Lord, 'I cry to you and you give me no answer . . . you have grown cruel in your dealings with me.' And God answered him: 'Where were you when I laid the earth's foundations? Have you ever given orders to the morning?' Then Job laid his finger on his lips: 'I have been holding forth on marvels beyond my knowledge.'

Poor old Job, you didn't solve the problem, you simply shut your eyes and gave up. But it isn't easy to follow in your footsteps. Let's try the Gospels. On the way to Caesarea Philippi Peter declares to Jesus: 'You are the Son of the living God', and Jesus replies that he will have to suffer, die and rise again. What a mysterious bundle of contradictions!

Then there's the Revelation of St John: blood and death, lions' mouths and scorpions' tails tormenting people, martyrs bathed in blood – it's all quite sinister. Then all at once there comes a change of tune: the sweet sound of harpists, gaiety and joy; weeping, wailing, hardship and death have disappeared for ever. God himself wipes away all tears from their eyes. 'The holy city, new Jerusalem' comes down from God out of heaven 'prepared as a bride adorned for her husband'.

Yes, but what of this world? Are those lines by Voltaire? (I'm quoting from memory)

On entre, on crie,
Et c'est la vie;
On baille, on sort,
Et c'est la mort.

We are born – a cry – a yawn – we die.

Is that really all there is to man?

Here, in this country of deep religious faith, Christians and Muslims speak in another language: when they talk of death, particularly that of a child, they frequently look up at the sky: *'And Rabbuna* – he is with God.' Even the mothers point up at the eternally clear sky. 'He's gone to a better place,' they murmur through their tears.

In one swift stride these simple-hearted women penetrate the veil that shrouds the mystery. The words of Christ on childbirth reverberate deep inside them. They have so frequently given birth to the child of their joy in pain. They are confident that the small, stiff body in their arms is an angel calling them to the happiness of the life hereafter.

And I, when my heart falters in the face of human pain, I think of Pascal's wager: should I opt for a nonsensical world and climb astride the pale horse of the Apocalypse with death riding pillion and men and children perishing without hope in the abyss? Or should I leap on to the white horse with Christ, to be borne in spirit amongst a great host of people singing for joy and happiness?

I decided to back the white horse. It's my favourite colour.

Marie-Paule

It was 6.30 on a Monday morning, and in the peaceful little chapel of the Carmelites, mass was beginning. The Sisters could be glimpsed, dressed all in white, sitting on their little stools. One of them came forward to the grille and read with an unfaltering voice a passage from the prophet Isaiah: 'The desert shall rejoice, and blossom as the rose. It shall blossom abundantly and rejoice even with joy and singing.'

With open hands, I offered up my shanty-town to the Lord. Who would come and help me make it rejoice and blossom? The prioress, whom I saw from time to time always questioned me with interest about my work. I knew that behind those grilles those devout women were still receptive to the world and its problems, and were calling upon the Lord. Would they reach Mount Carmel like the prophet Elijah, and cause the rain to fall, making the desert blossom, and our ragpickers along with it?

Someone came up to me: 'Marie-Paule is waiting for you.'

' – ? – '

The girl from the Grail next door. The Grail is an institution that has spread throughout the world. Its name reminds one of the legend of Parsifal, the medieval knight who went in search of the Holy Grail, the mysterious chalice in which the blood of Christ was preserved. I don't know all that much about it, but I visualize these new Parsifals setting off across the continents as modern knights to spend the treasures of their brains and their hearts for the benefit of their fellow men – it's quite an appealing idea, with a touch of mystique for the uninitiated like myself.

I went in search of my twentieth-century Parsifal and found myself confronted by a charming young girl in trousers who said to me without preamble: 'I'm interested in the ragpickers. Can I go and see them?'

'Of course, I'm off there myself for the week.'

With packs on our backs we jumped on a train and away we went across . . . the desert.

'This is just what I've been dreaming of. Can I stay here with you?' exclaimed Marie-Paule, when we arrived. The street was piled high with filth and swarming with children dressed in rags.

Make yourself at home. My house is yours.

We went inside my shanty. 'There is just enough room for two small planks next to your bed, Sister.'

'All right.'

Fleas, cockroaches, spiders, rats – nothing could deter her. We slept peacefully side by side.

Soon she was much loved in the shanty-town and she spent several months helping me in the kindergarten in the mornings and with the girls in the afternoons. In the evenings she benefited from the young teacher Ali's instructions in the alphabet, and he was delighted to have this fresh-faced girl among his rough and ready pupils.

Marie-Paule had studied child care and was interested in babies, particularly Fauzeya's. 'Echref and Sobhi, *ta 'ála héna*, come here.' There were shouts and laughter; flowers of joy were blooming in the desert.

'What I want is simply to share, to live with them, as one of them.' She had other friends, who invited her to one or the other of their comfortable apartments in the attractive part of Cairo. But she always came back to share our shanty-town, with the same smiling face.

One day, however, I found a change in her. She was looking on the dark side of everything. We were not achieving anything. What was the good of sending them to school when they didn't want to study? 'It's no use. In two days everything will be just as dirty again,' she remarked while she was helping me with the spring cleaning. What had gone wrong? Things had gone so wrong that she was obliged to stop work with raging fever. She was haemorrhaging and her stomach was all churned up.

The doctor was worried and ordered her to be taken to the clinic for tests. They found some bacteria. I went to see her, and found her room festooned with flowers and multicoloured balloons. 'Look how kind the people from the Grail were to me on my birthday.' Once again she was wreathed in smiles. 'As soon as I'm better, I shall share in the life of the ragpickers again,' she added.

You were brave, Marie-Paule, you went to the very limits of sharing – beyond them even. I warned you never to accept anything but a glass of tea that had been boiled, but you wanted to share the same plate too. Young people don't know the meaning of the word discretion. To them, love has no fear of death. Oh for the heart of a young person!

She came calmly back to live amongst us but then war broke out with all the uncertainty of what the next day would bring. The consulate insisted that she should return to France and her friends put pressure on her to leave. So in the end she bought her ticket.

'What do you think about all this?' she asked when she came to see me. 'It's not very nice to get out when the going is dangerous. I wanted to share the danger but my parents are panicking!'

She came to the shanty-town for one last time. I had never seen her cry but, confronted by the grief of Fauzeya and her children, she could no longer hold back the tears.

Marie-Paule had always told me that she was not interested in God and religion, but a letter arrived with a quotation from St John: 'Beloved, let us love one another; for love is of God.' She added quite simply: 'I am happy.'

People of good will follow two paths which may eventually converge. One leads from a rapturous vision of God to a tender regard for mankind. The other leads from our fellow men to a discovery of the Father who is in heaven. St John, with his eagle eye, saw through the clouds and added to what Marie-Paule wrote to me: 'Every one that loveth is born of God.'

4. Sharing

Pulex irritans

I consulted learned books on entomology in search of accurate information about one of the smallest creatures in existence: the flea. I don't know why, but it seems to have a particular affection for rag-pickers, myself included. The last volume I laid hands on, which was so fat that I could hardly lift it, gave this precise definition: 'Apterous insect, capable of running and jumping [as if I hadn't noticed], which lives [alas!] on the bodies of humans and a large number of animals.'

I next discovered that its eggs were a pearly grey (how poetic!), that from these emerged larvae equipped with masticatory organs (amazing!), that the larvae spun themselves a cocoon and that eventually after twenty days a 'perfect' insect would emerge. I could just see my entomologist bending lovingly over this perfect creature, noting next with evident interest that: 'The young flea can fast for from one to two weeks [my heart bleeds for it], waiting for a favourable moment to take on its supply of blood [after so long a fast, anything goes!].'

There followed a series of names for this creature turned bloodthirsty through sheer necessity: *Pulex irritans*, that was more like it! Our worthy author referred us then to an article on 'Pests', because he obviously didn't want to be responsible for charging so fascinating an insect with too many crimes. He merely noted in passing that it could also transmit miliary fever and '*dipylidium caninum*'.

Finally he provided a friendly word of advice for

the benefit of anyone who might have been startled by such harsh words. 'Where there is an abundance of fleas, one need only wrap oneself in a horseblanket that has been in use for some time . . .' If he had only added 'a pig blanket', I could have sorted myself out there and then, but where was I supposed to find a horse?

I had come to the end of my research, when I came across an advertisement in an old journal: 'Flea-collar for dogs. Guaranteed for three months.' At last, there was the answer! Delighted with my find, I spread the good news about. 'That's all you need! Don't forget the medallion with your name on it.' Never mind the jokes, I would wear it as a belt. I was just about to set off on a fund-raising expedition. I would make inquiries in Paris about this important item.

A few days later a friend arrived and announced triumphantly: 'I've cut you an advertisement out of a newspaper: a Dutchman wants live fleas. He's offering a pound a head. You can guarantee the success of your journey in advance. Take a good supply with you!'

Yâ saláam! In my suitcase? How? They'd escape, and after twenty days and one or two weeks of fasting their offspring would make lovely visiting cards! But I did add a reminder to my notes for the journey: 'Paris, flea-collar'. Traipsing from shop to shop, I chanced upon a store in the Hotel de Ville: 'In the basement, Sister.' The salesgirl gave me all the patter: 'It's effective and it's guaranteed.' She even knew someone who had used one (someone like the son of her sister-in-law's cousin) and been very pleased with it. I was convinced.

'How much is it?'

'Thirty-five francs.'

The figure sent a chill down my spine. To the ragpickers that amount of money meant food for a family for several weeks. I left, deep in thought. No, really, how could I claim the right to buy myself such a luxury? Either I was a ragpicker or I wasn't! I must make up my mind who I was. I left the store chuckling to myself: 'Friends must share everything, even *pulex irritans.*'

The maggots

It had been tipping it down in one of those great winter downpours that transform our narrow streets into cesspools, ankle deep in mud. Most of the children stayed away from school, but some of the older girls turned up in the afternoon, mud-bespattered and laughing. Sabrina, our wonderful doll, was the prize for so much courage. She was passed, don't let's say from hand to hand, but from heart to heart because each child squeezed her tightly to her chest and then covered her with tender kisses.

I was called out to a sick baby, and my little girls were concerned for me. '*Ableti*, big sister, you will slip over in the mud.'

'No, I won't, you're going to help me.' They grabbed my hand and off we went.

When I went into my hut that evening, I was horrified to see whole cohorts of white maggots wriggling about on the ground. They were slithering from all directions under the board that served as a wall and writhing about in a squirming mass. Where were they coming from? I went outside and found a pile of muck dumped in front of the door, swarming with them in their thousands. No doubt the rain had put new life into them and they were on a reconnaissance expedition — the scouts were already in my home.

I tried to stop my tide of visitors with DDT powder, boiling water and petrol. They seemed to make for the guttering like rats, flouting me even as they squirmed. I lost the battle and was beginning to lose heart. What if they climbed on to my bed and attacked me during the night?

I summoned my friend Labib, who came in and looked at them, then at me. Then with a quiet, philosophical air, he inquired: 'Why are you frightened? Aren't these the same maggots that will be with us when we are laid under the ground?'

I stood there gaping. What sage or philosopher could have given me an answer like that?

I went to bed, telling myself: 'He's right, it's only a question of sooner or later!' But not one of them set foot on my skin during the night. The following day the sun was shining, the army had left as it had come. When would we meet again?

The rats

The animal which is naturally most at home where we are, and which multiplies rapidly, is the rat. It has almost become domesticated. Lodged comfortably in some piece of rag under the bed, it's for ever poking out its nose, running between your legs and leaving you a last view of its long twisted tail. Its bright eyes will soon spot the water in a pan left on the ground. It will trot over to it, lap up the beverage with relish and disappear, leaving a little for the next one who fancies it, be he man or beast.

In the early days I used to shudder every time one appeared, much to the amusement of my neighbours. 'But don't they ever bite you?' I asked them.

'Of course they do, just take a look at Chehta's nose!' Pointed teeth had left their mark.

A little while later I was treating Ramadan's finger which had three pointed holes in it. The animal must have been a good size. I couldn't help thinking of bubonic plague. 'Go straight to the doctor, Ramadan. You know he only comes here on Fridays, and it's Monday today.'

'Just because of a rat?' he shrugged his shoulders.

His finger healed and he didn't catch the plague.

Om Mervat admitted to me that she was a little

disconcerted when the rats walked about on her face at night.

'Why don't you keep a cat?' I suggested naively.

She burst out laughing. 'The rats catch the cats here; haven't you noticed how big and fat they are?'

Once again I found myself disarmed. The most ostensibly simple problem turned out to be insoluble.

Not being equipped with the same capacity for endurance, I can't get used to their visits. I diligently stop up the holes they are for ever making in the earth floor of my hovel. An expert on the subject advised me to put some pieces of glass in the holes; apparently that dampens their ardour. It so happened that the glass in my paraffin lamp had broken again and I hadn't yet thrown the pieces away. Now was my chance. I carefully made up some little sandwiches filled with rat poison, and crammed them into all the holes which I stopped up with cement and glass. I did actually have some peace for a while. But then, one morning, to my horror, I saw a rat's dropping on my sheet. There was no mistaking it; we had spent the night together. I dived under the bed: a long open tunnel plunged into goodness knows where. But now I had the recipe of an expert with a broken lamp: sandwiches, cement, glass – good-bye my little friends!

The ragpickers watched me knowingly out of the corners of their eyes. 'Don't wear yourself out. Those rats are more cunning than you are, they'll be back to visit you by some other route.' We laughed together.

The following night I saw a rat at the skylight of my hovel taunting me through the grating. 'See you soon!' it seemed to say. I banged on the wall with my fist and it disappeared . . . Oh for the stolidity of the ragpickers!

Part of the Incarnation

The bus moved slowly forward, then came to a stop.
A crowd was waiting on the pavement. More people
stormed their way aboard until we found ourselves
packed like sardines in a tin. We stood on one leg
like herons, while the other wobbled about unable to
find solid ground. All that moist flesh was giving off
a stifling smell. Hello! someone was getting up in
first class. He had been sitting next to the window.
Marvellous! 'Sister Ghislaine, quick, go and sit
down,' I called to my colleague. She didn't move and
the seat was taken.

Getting off was another major operation. "An iznak.
Permit me.' We pushed to the left, then to the right,
ducked under a soldier's arm, edged sideways
between a hundred kilos of matron and the heavy
bulk of a boxer, in an attempt to get out alive.
Khallas! Saved! We got our breath back. The com-
pressed balloons of our lungs filled out again and we
walked along the street, full of the joys of living.

'Good morning, Sister.' A little tot of five years old
came up and shook us effusively by the hand.
'Ezzayek, how are you?' smiled his mother.

Wherever we went we met with the same joy on
the children's faces, the same expansive welcome
from their parents. 'You're beginning to be loved
here, Sister Ghislaine. How many do you have in
your kindergarten?'

'A hundred and thirteen according to the register
the day before yesterday.' Exactly one year ago, she
had started with thirteen.

'Tell me, why didn't you want to go and sit in first
class? An extra piastre wouldn't have been the end
of the world! You must be tired out.'

There was a moment's silence. 'To me, it's the
Incarnation.'

'I don't quite understand.'

'Don't you see? Christ came amongst us with our

77

human flesh, our poor human flesh. When I find myself squashed like that in the middle of all those people, I feel human in the fullest sense of the word, like him. I am closer to him than if I went and sat in first.'

Words failed me. For nearly all her life, Sister Ghislaine had been a headmistress and Superior in our large schools, with a telephone in her office and a car at the door. She had only to call the lodge: 'I have to go out in a few minutes, please tell the chauffeur,' before leaving in a constant rush for some important meeting or other. Naturally she had only to sit down in the refectory and, as Superior, she would be served immediately. Her clothes used to be waiting for her each morning, washed and ironed, in her room where not a speck of dust was ever to be seen.

Now if you're invited to our little apartment in Matareya and you ring at the door, she will open it with a smile, in her apron. She has just finished sweeping up. This evening, before she goes to bed, she will do the laundry. Here she is now, in the middle of her horde of little urchins, surrounded by the people she loves. She has just started a course in dress-making for the women. She also intends to set up a first-aid and child-care centre for them, and for the children crammed into overcrowded rooms she plans to provide a place where they can study undisturbed in the evening. For her, all this is again part of the Incarnation.

Prayer

I still have a lot to learn from my Coptic brothers. It is they who set me back on the straight and narrow when necessary.

In the early days, my life with the ragpickers had become a series of interrupted activities: when I got back from early morning mass it was straight to the little ones, then it was care of the sick, lunch, the girls, then instruction in the alphabet until ten o'clock at night, supper, bed and the same again next day. My time for prayer was taken up in other duties. Only on Sunday mornings, spent in the Carmelite chapel, did I have the opportunity to pray, read and meditate on the Bible. Then I immersed myself in the inexhaustible mine of the language of biblical theology, but during the week I really didn't give it much time.

One day Abou Labib, the owner of my hovel, asked me straight out: 'Betsalli emta? When do you pray?'

'In the mornings at mass, and on Sundays.'

'Is that all. Aren't you a rahba? a nun, a woman of prayer?'

This devout man gave me food for thought. When it actually came down to it, what was I really? A social worker during the week and a nun on Sundays? In my confusion, I sensed that my neighbours, up to their necks in garbage, expected something different from me. How many times had they said to me with a sigh, 'Pray for me'. I recalled a picture from my childhood which I had found so romantic and beautiful – St Geneviève keeping night watch over Lutèce. First and foremost, my indigent friends regarded me as their ambassador to the Lord. After that, of course, there was nothing to stop me looking after their children, their paperwork and their bruises.

I also remembered L'Ame de tout apostolat, a book from my youth which isn't fashionable any more either. In it Dom Chautard cited the fact that the active life must stem from the contemplative life as the most important principle.

'I'm going to pray,' I said to Fauzeya. 'Tell people not to disturb me unless it's absolutely necessary.' I closed the door of my hovel, lit the paraffin lamp and stayed there silently with Christ, offering up to the Lord the world and all its ragpickers.

'*Alrahba, maoguda*? Is the Sister there?' said a voice outside.

'*Aiwa betsalli*. Yes, she's praying, come back in a little while.'

'*Kwayyess*. All right.'

The visitor went away, happy that the Sister was praying. God was not far from the ragpickers.

Ramadan and his radio

One day Ramadan came to work with us. He was fifteen years old, with a bronzed face and fiery eyes. Where was he to sleep? The piglets and their mother were moved out of their sty and the place was ready. Ramadan could sleep there safely.

'Do you know why I'm here?' he confided. 'My father lent some money to a man who didn't want to pay it back. So what else could my father do but kill him? He's still in prison. "You're fifteen now," my mother said to me, "the son of the murdered man will try to kill you. Go away somewhere . . ." So here I am!'

He laughed, exposing a set of large white teeth. It seemed quite natural to him to have to run away from a killer. That killer would be given ten pounds for every blow dealt successfully. It wasn't a bad line of work; particularly when the maize was ripe, it was easy to strike a man down.

'But my mother isn't stupid!' He snapped his fingers with delight!

In the evenings he would come back early and stretch himself out on the straw because there wasn't really anywhere else to go or anything much to do. One day he arrived with a cracked old radio which he played at full blast. There I was in my hovel trying to pray, but a rasping voice drowned me out with its raucous cries. I went out and reproached my young neighbour: 'Listen, Ramadan, I'm going to pray now.

80

Would it be too much to ask you to turn your radio down a little?'

'Na'am, na'am.'

I went back inside and sat down. There was total silence. Now what? Out I came again: 'Ramadan, what's up? Why have you switched off your radio?'

'Because you're praying to God.'

'You don't have to do that, Ramadan, I can pray quite easily while you're listening to your radio. Turn it on.'

'No, no, I'm tired. I'd rather go to sleep.'

There was nothing I could do to convince him otherwise. I went back to my prayers but with a somewhat heavy heart. Ramadan's old radio was his only source of entertainment and because of me he was depriving himself of even that pleasure. What a sensitive soul this young Muslim was! Prayer was sacred, there was no way he would wish to obstruct it.

Since that time, whenever the radio is blaring away, I slip stealthily into my hovel and offer up to the Lord the cries of the world.

Mahmoud

Mahmoud lives on the same floor as the sisters in our little apartment in Matareya. I bump into him sometimes on Sundays when he goes off to work in his immaculate white *djellabir*. When he got married, he asked permission to light up our little balcony which adjoins his, a sign of popular rejoicing that can be seen daily throughout the town. On Thursday evenings in the squares strings of yellow, red and blue lights are lit while shrieks of joy ring out in fits and starts. The night is taken up with singing and dancing, even though men and women are kept rigorously apart in the crowd and only the girls and boys from progressive families dance together. At dawn everyone leaves to take advantage of a day off on Friday to recuperate.

Mahmoud's brother, Moustapha, is one of the Lord's greatest football players. As soon as he gets back from high school, textbooks and exercise books are dumped on the bed and he's off like a shot to join in the heated game which goes on without interruption underneath our windows. Every now and then disputes break out over some dubious shot.

A few days ago a scuffle turned sour and began to degenerate into a battle. Mahmoud, who is stronger and stockier than his young brother came to his rescue, but the fury of the assailants only increased. One of them picked up a sharp stone and, with unerring aim, threw it at Mahmoud's head. He collapsed. Blood spurted out in floods from a wide gash in his skull and his white *djellabir* was stained with traces of red which interlaced in an Arabesque pattern and poured on to the dust. Quick as a flash the football players vanished into thin air, only to be replaced by the district's women and youngsters yelling at the top of their voices. There were police and ambulance sirens — Mahmoud was taken to hospital half-conscious, put on a white bed and given compresses and glucose.

After five days he was brought home to convalesce for a further two weeks. I went to see him while he was still pale and weak, and he told me the details of this little drama.

'What about the person who got you into this state, did the police pick him up?' I asked, appalled.

'No, I didn't want to give his name.'

'But, Mahmoud, he'll do it again to someone else!'

Weakly, he shook a head still swathed in bandages. A smile passed over his tired features so that they suddenly shone with love: 'No, no, I won't give him up, he didn't know what he was doing.'

Two thousand years ago, a strangled voice raised from a body dying on a cross: 'Father, forgive them, they know not what they do.' Now I had heard its echo in the mouth of a man who knew nothing of the drama of Calvary. The Holy Spirit blows where he will.

Sharing

At that time I was staying in the apartment in Matareya getting ready for our holiday camp.

'On Sunday I shall be getting in some *halawa* [a cheap, nutritious paste made out of oil and sesame seeds which was not currently available in the markets]. Shall I keep three kilos back for you?' asked the grocer on the corner.

'Please do.' What luck!

My three kilos arrived in a long sausage which I examined with interest. I was stocked up with food to fortify me for a long time. But what about the others? I thought of the numerous families who bought their fifty grams or so daily and who would have to do without because of my sausage. I had let myself be talked into it, without thinking . . . Come on, old girl, what are you going to do about it? Take the sausage back? Ah! the camp! My little ones would love to eat a nice *halawa* sandwich every now and then, and it would do them good.

In the meantime, what a vigilant watch I must keep on myself to make sure that I shared not only fine talk, air and sun, but the material goods of this life. I had just read those terrible words of St Basil and they had engraved themselves on my mind: 'The bread which remains unused in your home belongs to one who goes hungry; the garment hanging in your wardrobe belongs to one who is naked; the shoes which remain unused in your home belong to the poor barefoot beggar; the money you keep tucked away belongs to the poor. You commit as many injustices as you could distribute kindnesses.'

I opened my wardrobe. There wasn't much in it,

but that overall was no use to me because I had
another. Come on now, it would make that wife and
mother happy. Her own was full of holes. Well, St
Basil, what about that?

There was a whisper in my ear: 'Have a look at
your woollens.' Good, there was a white shawl I had
been given to wear when I went out at night.

'Basil, you're frowning! What are you growling
about, old saint?'

'You have a black one for when you go out during
the day. Do you really need a white one to go out at
night?'

'You're right, Basil, Fauzeya shall wrap her baby
in it. But that's all, isn't it?'

'Hm, what about those thick socks?'

'Don't get carried away, Basil. I've only just been
given those as a present. You know it's bitterly cold
at night in the shanty-town. In winter I risk catching
a cold or bronchitis, broncho-pneumonia, my death!
Doesn't that mean anything to you?'

'What about your old socks?'

'They're to be thrown out!'

'Mend them, my girl, mend them. They'll do. And,
above all, don't forget to keep the old ones for
yourself and give the new ones away!'

There's no *modus vivendi* with these saints. Om
Makram had tears in her eyes when she put on the
thick socks. 'They'll ease my rheumatism. If you only
knew how I suffer!'

January brought winter with all its callous cruelty.
Snuggled under my two covers, I didn't suffer
unduly, but when I stepped outside my hovel I found
Fauzeya white with cold: 'It was terrible last night,
we were all shivering.' As is usual here, the whole
family slept in the one bed. I went inside. I should
really have noticed before: all they had to cover them
was a kind of patchwork sheet.

What would you have done, you who are reading
this, warm and cosy at night under your soft blankets?

The approach to Sister Emmanuelle's house at Ezbet el Nakhl.

Zabbaleen children in the new kindergarten.

Street houses in Ezbet el Nakhl.

Sister Emmanuelle and a Zabbaleen family.

Ezbet el Nakhl, the "shantytown" where Sister Emmanuelle
lived and worked.

Some of the children of Ezbet el Nakhl.

At the moment, of course, you're not thinking of sharing them with a stranger lying helpless, perished with cold, several hundred kilometres away. But imagine for one instant that only a plank separates you from a family of small children who are shivering with cold and whom you will soon hear coughing in the night. Could you sleep comfortably in the warm? Impossible! You would call their mother and say: 'Look, I have two covers, take the larger one. I'll sort something out.' And without further ado, you would fold the remaining one in half, sew a few bits of cloth on either side so that you could tuck yourself in nicely and then you would be able to snore away to your heart's content. And what's more, Basil would give you his blessing!

The bonfire

A good cutting knife is a precious commodity for us. I have one. The other day a woman came rushing in: 'Quickly, quickly, your knife.'

'Just a minute, just a minute, I'm in the middle of giving the children a lesson.'

'No, no, straight away!'

I gave it to her and she ran off. A few moments later she returned it to me sadly: 'It's too late, he's dead.' She left as she had come.

I was a little concerned. 'Fauzeya, what was all that about the knife and a death?'

Fauzeya looked serious: 'Oh yes, that poor woman lost her pig!'

'—?—'

'When you see that an animal is very sick, you have to kill it quickly and then you can use its meat, but if it's already dead, it's no good, it has to be thrown away. It's quite a loss, don't you see?'

I wasn't too sure about those dying pigs, killed at the very last minute. I went out into the alleyway. The animal had been thrown on the muck heap. In a very short time it promised to provide us with a delicious aroma, flies, germs and company. We should pour paraffin over it. It wouldn't cost much and it would avoid a multitude of ills. The youngsters, delighted with this novel idea, clustered round me. The liquid seeped through the dark bristles. A match was struck and the animal went up in flames. The little urchins danced and sang around it. What a magnificent bonfire!

We went back to sit in the classroom on our best behaviour and I explained why it was necessary to burn dead pigs, dogs and donkeys, cats and rats. The children listened attentively. A few days later, I came across a charred carcass. Thank God, this time the lesson had sunk in!

On the following day I saw a gathering of people and went over to it. A kind of butcher who seemed to be an expert in the field was in the throes of cutting up a donkey. 'Look at that lovely meat!'

Would our man sell it as beef cutlets and stew? That I'll never know!

A knife and a bar of soap

I loan out 'my' famous knife very cautiously and keep a close eye on it. Every time Fauzeya asks me for it, I hand it to her with the hallowed instruction: 'Don't forget to bring it back.' After all, it's 'my' one and only knife. I'm its lawful owner.

Every now and then Fauzeya manages to produce a decent meal and when she does she happily brings me a little in a dish. I have never heard Fauzeya say to me: 'Don't forget to bring it back – it's "my" dish.' That woman is not at all possessive, her hands are always open.

One evening, at supper-time, I looked for 'my' knife but couldn't find it anywhere. I was worried. What! It wasn't there at 'my' disposal any more, as an object over which I was master?

'Fauzeya, do you have "my" knife?'

'Oh yes.' She foraged everywhere and found it under the bed. She rinsed it under the pump and brought it back to me, laughing mischievously: 'As we're sisters, shouldn't it be "our" knife?'

I looked at her, laughing in my turn and hugged her saying: 'You're right, but if you like, as the children are into everything and lose everything, we can let it live with me when you don't need it.' The matter was settled.

A few days later I stumbled on the words of St John Chrysostom: ' "My", that little word which is oh, so cold!'

The time had come to start the holiday camps for a succession of youngsters. I was quite annoyed because it was difficult to get hold of any soap during the aftermath of the war but just as I was leaving with my swarm of enraptured, squalling girls, a voice called out to me. Fauzeya came running up and stuffed two bars of soap into my bag. A short while ago she had had three bars on her bed.

'You can't do that, just give me one.'

'No, your need is greater than mine.'

My sister, Fauzeya, went back to her hovel in high spirits; on her bed, black with flies, in place of the two missing bars of soap she saw two pools of light.

5. Life at camp

The girls

Sister Ghislaine had lent us the two rooms she used for her kindergarten, which were vacant for the holidays, so that I could rescue our little ragpickers from the filth in turns.

For two months the camp had been the main topic of conversation among our girls. It would be those who had worked regularly and conscientiously every afternoon who would be allowed to go. They would stay at Matareya, surrounded by a large garden, they would go for lovely walks and – wonderful! they would each have a new little dress to wear during the day and a nightdress to go to bed in . . . As for the two little pairs of knickers (also new) they would each give me five piastres (five pence) and would have to learn how to make them: the knickers they would be able to take away with them after the camp, whereas the dresses and nightdresses would have to be left there for the following year.

Armed with money donated by generous friends, I went shopping with Sister P from Our Lady of the Apostles who is an expert at finding bargains. We came back with some reasonably priced light floral material, and able hands made up some simple but attractive little dresses and nighties.

The trying-on session was yet to come. Of course they all wanted to rush at once at such tempting materials. We are not daughters of Eve for nothing!

'*Yallah!* All right, everyone outside the door. You'll be called in one at a time.'

Because the ragpickers have preserved the customs

of Upper Egypt, even the little girls wear long dresses, but when it came to doing the hem, to my amazement, I heard our youngsters protesting: 'No, no, above the knee!'

Now we were in for it! 'Look, children, I don't want to go against your parents' wishes.'

In the end it was decided that the skirts should fall a fraction below the knee. That would keep both the girls and their mothers happy.

When we arrived at the camp each one was made to stand, shivering, under a shower. What was that? Rain in summer? A large thing like a ball! It won't fall on my head will it? Eventually their minds were set at rest and they were duly soaped from top to toe to get rid of their *pulex irritans* and any other residents. Clean underwear, a pretty dress, a ribbon in their neatly combed hair – it was marvellous to be clean in a clean place amongst clean people! Evening brought yet other delights: they went to bed in a nightdress, they each had their own little mattress, and when they fell asleep it was with Alice in her wonderland.

So that first day had passed like a dream. Astonished to see themselves looking so sweet, they stopped quarrelling and hitting each other, and I wondered how I could ever have had any reservations about the camp.

On the second day, things were still going well: writing, arithmetic and the basics, catechism for the Christians and morality for the Muslims, alternated with games, singing and good meals. But on the Wednesday morning when I got back from mass I sensed a change in the atmosphere. A suffocating Khamsin wind was blowing, the temperature would soon be nearly 40°C and the young monitress who was supposed to take them for gymnastics lacked experience. The little girls hadn't wanted to do as they were told so she had threatened to beat them. The girls responded with some of the choicest words from their vocabulary. Clean out of patience and at her wits' end, she had hurled the ultimate insult at them: 'It's quite obvious that you come from the garbage heap!'

Finding my little girls dejected and unhappy, I made them tell me what had happened and was filled with consternation. How deeply those children must have been wounded! I would have to teach that inexperienced monitress a thing or two. 'Try to appreciate how much damage it can do! Everyone is sensitive when it comes to race, religion or family background. If you call me a filthy swine that hurts me, but "those filthy French swine" will wound me to the quick. We are trying to do all we can to get them away from their garbage if only for a few days, and you go and throw them back in it!'

Fortunately Sister P, whose mother tongue is Arabic, found more delicate words to smooth things over a little, but with the help of the heat and the devil our children started to fight and call each other names again. I was heartbroken.

By a stroke of good fortune, a trip to the zoo had been planned for the Saturday, to round off the week. The unaccustomed sight of so many unfamiliar animals was so compelling that they forgot every-thing else and we took them home as planned, this time without incident. I announced the names of those who could come back on the following Mon-day: there were only about ten of them and they would have to give me their solemn promise that they wouldn't fight.

In this way we managed to get going a good educational exercise. Our children began to respect each other. They waited until everyone had been served instead of lunging at their plates, they did their utmost to make progress in their reading and arithmetic, they came of their own accord to ask me to wash their soiled dresses – an extraordinary innovation! Highly amused by the fact that the water came out of the tap all by itself – they didn't have to do any more pumping – they began to scrub with enthusiasm and learned how to drip-dry their little dresses so that they didn't come out crumpled; after all, they didn't have an iron in their shanty-town.

'Next year can we come to camp again?' the little rascals I hadn't been able to keep asked me, without any bitterness, when I next saw them. 'Of course,' I replied, 'because you are going to grow into little angels!'

They hugged me effusively. If nothing else, they were a little cleaner!

The transfiguration

On 6 August, the Feast of the Transfiguration, at the Carmelite mass I heard the words of the prophet Daniel. In his night-time visions in Babylon, he saw borne towards him on heavenly clouds, the mysterious 'Son of Man' – *Bar Nasha* in Aramaic; the Hebrew term *Ben Adam*, son of Adam, sounds more familiar to our ears – and makes us all feel involved.

The second lesson was a reading from Luke who, two hundred years later, was once again drawing us into the heart of the mystery: Jesus, *Bar Nasha*, as he himself liked to be called, was suddenly transfigured and a cloud overshadowed his three terrified disciples.

When mass had ended I stayed behind for a few moments to pray alone in the silent peace of this Carmelite oasis and meditate on the words of the Byzantine vespers: 'O you who love visions beyond rational thought, let us contemplate mystically the Christ who shines with divine rays and who makes his light to shine on our souls.'

How lovely it would be to build a tabernacle on Mount Tabor, as Peter suggested to Jesus, but, as Luke in his account adds somewhat indulgently, 'not knowing what he said'. And after they had come down from the mountain, Luke describes equally coolly the epileptic foaming and rolling about on the ground whom Jesus cured and 'delivered him again to his father'. Aren't those last words wonderful?

It was time to come down from my mountain. After the girls, came our little demons – the little urchin boys aged six to eight who, once the carts had returned home, spent their time in all kinds of set-tos and then came running to have their injuries treated.

When I arrived at the camp, they were just saying grace before their meal. Afterwards, sitting in a circle on the ground, with a good plateful of beans at their feet, they greeted me with a resounding 'Sa'ide' and ate heartily – very busy and very well behaved!

I watched these little wild plants that grow amidst the garbage. For a few days we had transplanted them in the garden of Eden, so that the love with which we surrounded them could gradually transform them.

It was this transfiguration which made the effort of coming down from the mountain worth while.

Daoud, the bandit

One little fellow in my street, who three years ago was no more than knee-high to a grasshopper, had gradually grown taller. Violent and quarrelsome, Daoud (David) had jet-black eyes, a small nose well set in a dark brown face and a rounded head which he carried with authority. I had never seen this youngster do as anybody told him. Like Jean de Nivelle's dog that made off whenever it was called, he had only to hear his father or mother calling 'Daoud' and he would be off as fast as his little legs could carry him. If by chance someone managed to catch him, he would struggle with a ferocity quite astonishing for so small a body and his yells suggested quite exceptional lungs.

When he was six years old, I had long discussions

with his parents about whether he should go to school. Once I had convinced them, I tackled Daoud. That was an altogether different story. I could approach him only when he was busy eating quietly, but then he was only interested in his salad and onions. Whenever this little wild cat heard the word 'school', the expression would trigger off an irresistible reaction from him and a flight across the garbage would follow.

For the last year I had arranged for some young *chammas*, deacons in the Coptic Orthodox church, to come and teach these little heathens, who were baptized but nothing else, their catechism. Daoud had agreed to come to my home to hear some nice stories about God and to receive a pretty picture. Apart from one or two punches aimed at his neighbours sitting to his left and right, and the odd kick directed under the table at the youngsters sitting in front of him, he kept relatively quiet.

When the young *chammas* discovered that I was going to hold a camp for our children, they suggested having one for their pupils. I agreed, but for no more than about fifteen because I felt that it was quite important that the walls were still standing after they'd gone. They showed me their list of proposed names: 'Oh, Oh! Daoud.' They were taking their life in their hands. But how could you resist those jet-black eyes which looked at you so imploringly while a persuasive little mouth promised solemnly to be as good as gold?

We walked through the tall maize in single file. Daoud, in shoes too big for him, pressed on with confidence. By delivering a powerful punch at anyone who wanted to go past him, he arrived at the railway station the clear winner. No one could set about him because this little eight-year-old had concealed a flick knife in the rolled-over top of his shorts: it wouldn't have been safe enough in his pocket.

Luckily Nader, who knows him, was keeping a watchful eye on him. The minute Daoud engaged in close combat with Guirguis, his rival, he separated them. The two little scoundrels collapsed exhausted side by side on the *nasira*, a mat made out of red and yellow straw, which covered the tiled floor of the room.

'We'll have a rest for the moment, but you'll see later, I've got what it takes to put you in your place,' Daoud threatened Guirguis with a menacing look.

Nader was not satisfied. He called Daoud over and, in the course of conversation, said to him, 'Look what a beautiful knife I have.'

'Oh, I've got one too.' Daoud delved in his shorts and proudly displayed his weapon. Nader wasted no time in seizing it, saying quietly 'It's forbidden at the camp, Daoud. I'll give it back to you when you get back.' But the child was deaf in that particular ear. In a furious rage, he rolled about on the ground and began to yell. Then suddenly, taking advantage of a moment when no one was looking, he charged over to the door which led out into the garden, pulled back the old bolt that locked it and bounded into the street.

That little boy would get lost. We were far from his shanty-town and, once he had gone astray in the teeming labyrinth of Matareya's streets, he would never get out again. Fortunately someone had seen him. A frantic pursuit ensued because – whoever would have thought it! – that particular little demon had hind's feet, instead of goat's hooves!

At last he was seized by the shorts and brought back, sobbing with rage. Luckily Sister Marie of the Nativity came to my assistance this time. Taking him gently in her arms she explained to him like a mother that he couldn't be allowed to hold on to a large knife. Slowly he calmed down, and when the whistle blew for them all to play together, he launched himself headlong into a game with Guirguis and his mates.

The following day, this budding bandit threw himself in rage at a youngster who had dared to insult him and would have strangled him if someone hadn't intervened in time. Furious at having the prospect of revenge slip away from him, he stormed about angrily and refused to eat: 'I'm not hungry,' he insisted. Already lusting after vengeance, he wasn't interested in anything else. He carried on screaming with the occasional sob. My old grandmotherly heart was moved by it but Sister Marie and the chammas insisted that he was kept away from the others for a little while.

In the end I went over to him: 'Daoud, you see the chapel on that little hill? You've never been there, come and have a look at it.' Intrigued, he got up and clambered determinedly up a path obstructed by thorny brambles.

'Those thorns hurt.'

'When you hit people, that hurts them far more.'

He made no reply. We arrived outside the locked door of the old chapel.

'Now we're outside God's house, we're going to pray together. Are you a Christian, Daoud?'

He answered me with an emphatic nod of the head.

'And what did Jesus do for you, Daoud?'

His lips remained tightly sealed.

'He carried his cross and he asked us to love one another Abuna elazi fissamawat . . . Our Father, who art in heaven,' I began, and he prayed with me.

'That's it, Daoud, you're going to be a proper little Christian now!'

We came back down from our mountain and he went off quietly to play with his friends, looking somewhat calmer.

The next day the devil had got into him again. This time Melêk took him to a church where a service was being held in preparation for the feast of the Blessed

Virgin (22 August in the Julian Calendar and not 15 August as in the Gregorian). Daoud's little soul allowed itself to be uplifted by those ancient Coptic chants which are so very penetrating. On the way out he was given a roll of bread that had been blessed – 'Korban'. He shared it round the camp.

'What about Guirguis?' (his enemy of only a short time previously).

He rushed over to him, gave him a big piece and a kiss.

We had decided to take our little group to the zoo. Guirguis and Daoud, now reconciled, were holding hands as we stood in front of two monkeys in a cage. One of them, the stronger of the two, was grabbing the peanuts quickly and threatening to fight his mate if she made any attempt to take any of them. The female sat down on the floor of the cage, dejected.

'She's crying,' said Daoud.

'See how naughty the other one is, Daoud,' I pointed out. 'He's keeping them all for himself.'

After we had left I found some peanuts still in my pocket.

'There you are, Daoud, but don't do what the monkey did.' I left them with him.

We sat down to wait for the boat that would take us back across the Nile to the opposite bank and Daoud took out his packet of peanuts. I watched him without his noticing. He took one and ate it – charity quite properly begins at home – and then? Then, he handed one to each of the others; but he gave Guirguis two.

It was terribly hot, 30°C in the shade, and we were parched on the journey back to the camp. Daoud had been promoted to leader of a group of five youngsters. He had gone to buy the tickets at the station ticket office and solemnly distributed them amongst his group. We went into a store where they sold sugar cane juice.

'Daoud, you can hand out the glasses, and when everyone else has theirs, then you can take yours.'

The waiter held out four glasses. Daoud was terribly thirsty. He grabbed the first one and dipped his lips into it. Then, remembering his role as leader, he gave it to someone else and handed out the three remaining glasses. Busy with another group, I saw the waiter bring out one more glass.

'Who hasn't had a drink yet?'

Daoud put up his hand but then one of his friends called out: 'No, you've had some.'

Daoud pursed his lips, leaned his head on the counter and said nothing. Tears glistened in his eyes but still he said nothing.

'Daoud, it's yours.' He grabbed it and gulped it down in one go.

All conscientious Copts fast in preparation for the feast of the Blessed Virgin and our *chammas* saw to it that our meals included no meat, milk or cheese, but I noticed that they were very concerned that the children shouldn't be deprived of anything.

On the last day of the camp the children went to church again and in a final prayer they promised the Lord to love everybody and to honour their fathers and mothers.

A few days later I saw my young catechists again.

'We've just come back from the ragpickers and something extraordinary has happened: Daoud hasn't been in a single fight, he hasn't insulted anybody. He even said to his mother: "We must fast before the feast and tomorrow, Sunday, I have to go to church." He collected up all his friends and took them off to mass.'

Daoud, my little wolf turned lamb, I don't know whether, if your character is given a free rein, you will one day revert to being a bandit with a knife hidden in your belt; but once a man has met Christ in his childhood he can never forget him. One day, my little Daoud, you will hear those beautiful words, said two thousand years ago to a real bandit: 'Today thou shalt be with me in paradise.'

The five chammas

Chammas, one of the loveliest Coptic expressions, conjures up visions of a server in church who, dressed in a long white robe and red stole, stands in the chancel singing the sacred versicles at the top of his voice and taking an active part in the liturgy. Sometimes you come across little boys of five or six, especially the sons of celebrants, looking serious and meditative, already little budding deacons.

It should be noted in passing that no Coptic Orthodox priest can be ordained unless he is married. Having reached the final stages of his preparation for the priesthood, he finds a wife, leads the life of a married man for a few weeks and then goes to a monastery to prepare himself for ordination. Only the bishops, who are selected from among the monks, have to be unmarried.

The camp, run by the five *chammas* who had devoted themselves to it body and soul, was drawing to an end. Our little rogues hadn't always given them much peace at night. Sometimes they had had to put a stop to nocturnal battles, so they were tired and pale, and yet they said to me: 'What a shame the camp is over. It has done the children so much good.' But then one of them was leaving for Germany, another was going back to work, a third was getting ready for university entrance.

They were particularly insistent that Sister Marie and I should go and visit their families. For these devout people the presence of a person who has been consecrated to God brings a *baraka* with it. So it was that we found ourselves sitting in a small drawing-room decorated with pictures of Christ and the Virgin Mary. We chatted as we drank our strawberry syrup, and one particularly burning question was brought

out from under the carpet (or rather the floorboards
– in summer the carpets are put away – otherwise, I
suppose, they would only add to the prevailing heat).

'Are you going to take Muslims to the next camp
as well?'

'Yes, of course. I love Muslims as much as I do
Christians. Doesn't the Lord love them too?'

'They'll never go to Paradise.'

'Why not?'

'Because it is written in the Gospel that except a
man be born of water and of the Spirit, he cannot
enter into the Kingdom of God. Don't you believe
what it says?'

'Yes, but you must understand what is really meant
by the terminology: Is it water out of the tap? Or the
water of grace?'

'The water of grace, but its tangible sign is tap
water because man who has been endowed with
senses needs to see, hear and touch.'

'Fine, so when Christ refers to the streams of living
water which flow from the believer's heart is that still
the Nile coming out of the tap?'

'That's the water of grace, but you must do everything you can to see that everyone is baptized. Are
you a nun or a social worker?'

I thought for a moment and then said to them in all
honesty: 'No, my aim is not to have them baptized
but to help them to become people.'

'There you are, then, you're a social worker,' they
insisted.

The argument was a weighty one. 'Perhaps I'm
wrong, but with a clear conscience I believe I have to
love them unconditionally and not to use my services
to convert them to my religion.'

'You are only a channel, your role is to bring
people to Christ by letting his grace pass through
you.'

'You're absolutely right that I am only a channel.
As I see it, my role is to imitate Christ, by loving to

99

the limit, to the point of death if necessary. He will grant the light that he wants, when he wants. Young Muslims have come to me wanting to be baptized, and I have turned them down. They were quite put out but they were only twenty years old. 'You don't know what difficulties you will encounter,' I said to them. 'Finish your studies, be good to your families, help the poor and those who suffer, pray . . . and in two or three years, come back and see me.'

'You told them to help the poor, Sister. Can't you see, that's being a social worker again? Why didn't you give them some encouragement?'

'Because in all the Muslim countries I have passed through, I have come across numerous instances of young converts. It's too difficult, they end up breaking down. By teaching men to love one another, I draw them into the very heart of Christianity.'

There was a moment's silence. 'You must know Chapter 25 of St Matthew's Gospel: "I was hungry and thirsty, I was naked and you gave me food and drink and you clothed me. – Lord, we didn't know it was you, – No, but you did it to me." That passage is quite clear. It is not talking about a certificate of baptism, nor even about recognizing Christ, but about the service of our fellow men.'

It was getting dark and it was time to go. I suggested that we pray together as I knew it would give them all great pleasure. Facing east, as is the custom with them, we raised our hands: '*Abuna elazi fissamawat* . . . Our Father who art in heaven.' They accompanied us back very happily and an hour later they brought Sister Marie and me a picture of Christ praying in Gethsemane. On the back they had inscribed a quotation from the Acts of the Apostles: ' "They had all things in common" . . . Thanks be to our Lord Jesus who has granted us the opportunity for shared service in the vineyard of the Lord.'

We were both very deeply touched – how extraordinary it was that these young people already knew how to find their joy, labouring in the vineyard of the Lord.

'One day, I hope that we shall all meet again in heaven,' I said to them with a smile. 'And I'm sure we shall meet our Muslim brothers there.'

'*Inshalla*! May it please God!' they laughed.

'You won't go to heaven'

The discussion with the young *chammas* suddenly brings to mind an incident which was similar but in reverse.

I was in Paris that year, when I received a letter from Switzerland, from one of my former Muslim pupils. 'Sister, I would like to see you about a serious matter. My husband has given me permission to make the journey. Let me know what date I can come.'

'Heaven only knows what difficulty she's in,' I thought. She had had the usual clashes with her mother-in-law before, and one day she had even gone back to her parents in exasperation. Her father had managed to arrange for the young couple to live on their own and everything had been restored to order.

She arrived looking young and pretty, with that gentle expression in her hazel eyes which was so characteristically hers. We hugged each other warmly.

'Is everything all right at home?' I asked with a touch of concern.

'Everything is fine. My husband is the kindest of men and my little daughter gets prettier every day.' She showed me a delightful photograph.

'So what's this serious matter you've come about?'

She looked at me slightly hesitantly. 'Well, I'm practising my faith more and more conscientiously, and finding an extraordinary happiness in it.' Her face was radiant. 'You know how fond I am of you!'

'It's reciprocal,' I laughed.

'Well,' she went on, 'I said to myself, it's just inconceivable that my former teacher, who is so greatly loved, shouldn't go to heaven. Only Muslims will enter Paradise. I've come to talk to you very seriously. You must study our religion.'

The hazel eyes gazed at me full of affection and supplication. How could I fail to be moved? 'I've already studied your religion. I've read the Koran in French and in Arabic with the help of a friend.'

'It's very beautiful, isn't it?'

'Yes, there are some passages which brought me light.'

'Didn't they convert you?'

'Not really, my sweet. I've found so much light in the Gospels, in the teachings of Christ.'

'Yes, we recognize him to be a great prophet too but Mahomet was sent by God to conclude and purify all previous revelations. He was the last and therefore the greatest of all the prophets.'

'That's your opinion,' I replied gently, 'but it's not mine, you see. I believe that God asks each one of us to follow his own light and to do as much good in this world as possible.'

'Yes, that's what you used to say.' But she went on heatedly. 'I so much want you to go to heaven.'

'I hope we both will.' I smiled at her.

We continued talking for some time, but I shall never forget the veil of sadness covering those pretty hazel eyes as they gazed at me for one last time. She embraced me tenderly, then disappeared.

We men close the door of heaven in each other's faces; it was a very good thing that Christ gave his life to open it to all 'men of good will'.

Fasting

Since I've been sharing the life of the Coptic Orthodox people, I have been obliged to practise fasting. They have remained faithful to the tradition of the first

Christians who chased away their demons by prayer and fasting. Our demons seem to wander about completely at liberty. I was constantly being asked if I was fasting: 'Enti sáyma?' as the hallowed expression goes. So, to avoid shocking them, I set about it.

Strictly speaking, one shouldn't eat anything until midday but I had to admit that I couldn't keep to that and work at the same time. 'That's not the most important thing, what matters is that you don't eat any animal produce,' they told me.

'That's all right.'

Following their example, I got used to feeding myself on beans, lentils, rice, sweet potatoes, dates, potatoes, and of course the wholemeal bread which represents nine-tenths of the poor man's diet. The most conscientious Copts – and they are numerous – actually fast for more than two hundred days of the year!

Our zealous *chammas* held the third camp just before 22 August, the Feast of the Assumption. Naturally we all fasted. One day I took our youngsters into the large garden of one of our foreign schools. The Sisters welcomed our little ragpickers as if they were their own children. The Sister Superior handed me a generous banknote, instructing me to: 'Spoil them thoroughly at the zoo.' She took me through to the refectory: the table was laden with butter, cheese, cold meats, bars of chocolate, and so on.

'There are no Copts amongst you?' I commented, somewhat surprised.

'But of course there are.'

'Aren't you fasting before the feast of the Virgin?'

The response was the age-old argument: 'We can't fast because we're working.'

I didn't want to pursue the matter. After all, my question had been rather indiscreet. It really wasn't any of my business. I went back to my little ones who were wolfing down their bean and jam sandwiches with great gusto.

It's important to recognize that everything must be done with proper understanding. When I first began to share the diet of the poor who hardly ever eat meat, I fell ill, so I said to myself: 'You really are an ass, my pathetic friend, it's beyond your strength and your capabilities.' Then I had the good fortune to meet an expert in Egyptian dietetics.

'You can give up meat quite easily,' he explained, 'on condition that you find a substitute for its protein: broad beans, lentils, haricot beans, rice and, above all, fish are less expensive than meat and they are excellent for protein. Add to that dark honey and *halawa* and the vitamins in tomatoes and fruit. There is only one thing I should warn you about – because this diet is so light, you will feel hungry more quickly, but substantially you will be just as well, if not better nourished.'

I followed his expert advice and, much to my own and everybody else's amazement, I am healthier now than I was before. People say, 'Pooh! fasting, it doesn't make sense!'

'It doesn't make sense for you, sir. As for madam, and her daughter, they fast in their own way.'

'Oh, that's for the sake of their figures.'

'Well, this is for the sake of the Lord. Everyone to their own choice. One man practises yoga to prepare his soul for the contemplation of God, another to cure the twinges in his stomach. That's what freedom is all about, my dear sir!'

My own experience was quite conclusive: fasting helps 'brother ass' not to overload himself with oats so that he can climb the path up Mount Carmel more easily. But everyone to their own choice. No two asses are the same!

'It's worth killing yourself for that'

We were getting ready for our fifth camp with two young and very keen organizers. As always, we had first to round up our campers. The best time was always around one or two o'clock when the men got back from their rounds. It was a question of extracting their permission by force: these youngsters have their uses and their parents only manage without them with difficulty.

'Abou Mahmoud, will you let us have your son this week?'

'For how long?'

'Only four or five days if you like.'

'What's he going to do with you?'

'First and foremost, he's going to enjoy himself. That young man is going to play ball.'

'He'll go to the zoo and ride on an elephant,' added Ezzat, the organizer.

Mahmoud listened in a subdued silence.

'Will you take me on the back of an elephant with him?' replied his father with a laugh. 'Go on, Mahmoud, ask your mother to put you in your clean *djellabir*.'

We carried on through the muck. Osiris, the sun god from the days of the Pharaohs, son of Geb, the earth, and Nut, the sky, was giving back the life he had been given by his father, Geb, in burning rays. I began to melt and Ezzat began to burn.

Nevertheless we had to press on. I supported my old arm on the strength of his youth. 'Actually, what we are doing now is really the best thing we can do for our little ones.'

'How do you mean?'

'Wearing ourselves out for them.'

Like so many other young people here, Ezzat is a deep soul 'You're right,' was his comment. 'Christ died for us.'

We had come face to face with Hanna (John) sitting in the middle of the muck.

'Where is your mother?' It would be easier to prise this one away because his sister, Ansaf, had come back from the previous camp full of enthusiasm. We entered the shade of the hovel.

'Oh yes, he can go,' laughed his mother. 'It'll do him good.'

We set off again. For two hours we went from street to street — from burning sun to burning sun. Each prolonged discussion concluded with a leap for joy. Small sun-tanned bodies rushed to the pump to wash themselves, then follow us.

The train arrived and we jumped on with relief. When at last we arrived at the camp, Ezzat and I sank on to a bench in a shady part of the garden.

'We may be all in, Sister, but look at those little ones.' They had already got hold of a ball and were playing football under the shade of a canopy of palm fronds. They were full of a new-found cheerfulness. 'It's worth killing yourself for that,' concluded Ezzat.

A speech

Dressed in clean clothes, our little ragpickers were sitting in a semicircle on a mat. The guests were privileged enough to have a seat.

Before starting the celebratory games, Ezzat, took the floor. Here is the speech he gave, copied down word for word, with all its Egyptian sensitivity:

> Before we begin this modest little celebration, I am happy and grateful to be able to talk to you about some of the things which have impressed themselves upon my friend Saad and me during our association with these small children.
>
> Life is hard enough and we don't believe in making it any harder for these children who are only just starting out on it. Up till now all they have received in life is disdain and rejection. For the first time I have seen what

suffering the disdain people have for them causes. This suffering and disdain has left its mark on their faces, giving them the look of those who are abandoned, despised, rejected, deprived of happiness, affection, love and even of life itself. These children who are branded with dirt through no fault of their own have become garbage collectors just to keep our houses clean, and in return society looks upon them with disdain and disgust.

I am speaking on behalf of these little ones who have been cut off from society and from life. Can we call ourselves their brothers and leave them in this predicament? A predicament which rules out all affection and expels innocent human beings from society itself?

I have not the words to convey what I saw on my first visit to the ragpickers but I did also notice the joy and happiness on their faces. So it is possible to make them partially forget the harshness of their life by giving of the best of oneself, by bringing them a heart full of love, affection, goodness, encouragement, comfort and the desire to live . . .

In conclusion, I would like to thank all those who have helped us to accomplish the Lord's work among these little abandoned souls . . . I am happy to see smiles and happiness etched on their faces thanks to what God has granted them to help make them blossom.

A smile

The camp was over, and we had returned some beaming little ragpickers to their parents.

'Shall we do it again?' they asked.

'Yes, one day we'll go for a nice outing, but mind there are no more fisticuffs and no more insults. Your mothers will be asked whether you have been behaving better!' We watched as our little urchins sat down on the ground at the centre of a circle paralysed with astonishment and recounted their adventures.

Adults and children rushed up to us from all directions to shake us by the hand. 'How's your wife?' I inquired. 'Is your little girl better? Is your elderly father still in hospital?' A smile here, a pat there, congratulations to a young mother, a telling off for some little fellow who was being insufferable, and we were off again through the maize which towered above our heads.

'What's the best thing you give the ragpickers, Sister?' Ezzat asked point-blank.

'The best thing, hmm! A cup of cocoa made with milk, courtesy of friends who get it for me. The children drink it with great relish.'

'No, no, Sister, it's something quite different. It's not a material thing.'

'Not a material thing?' I laughed. 'I give them my small heart. Is that a material thing or not?'

'Sister, what you give them is more precious than gold or silver. You give them your smile.'

A large stalk of maize had fallen across the path; my foot stumbled over it but Ezzat steadied me. 'Thank you, my friend. You were saying? Ah yes, my smile.'

'I noticed their faces when you smiled as you shook hands with them. A kind of dawn broke over them.'

'You're very poetic, Ezzat, but I have a wrinkled old face, you know. I don't light up any dawns. Look at Sister I, who came with us this week. Now she's young. That's quite different.' We all three began to laugh.

Ezzat wouldn't let his idea drop: 'Ibtisam, a smile, that's what people crave for. Throw a hundred pounds at them and that's worth nothing. Give them ten piastres with a smile, from your heart, and you've really made them richer.' Suddenly I thought of some of St Anthony's handouts of bread; people came and the bread was literally thrown at them . . . quick, on to the next one! That hurt! 'Ibtisam, ihtiram,' added Ezzat. 'A smile means respect, recognition of another's value, the first step towards making him a richer person.'

108

It was time for us to part company. It had been good working together to make our little ragpickers bloom. We said goodbye to each other – with a smile.

For what purpose?

During our last camp, joyful, hurrahs had made themselves heard from the other side of the little wall which divided into two the large garden of the Jesuit church. They were partly the result of a serious conversation with Father B.

'You are set here right in the heart of Matareya, Father. What are you doing for its people?'

'Yes, I've been thinking for a long time that we ought to take an interest in the people around us, open up this garden to children who have only the street to play in, organize some games and activities that will make them blossom out, give them a sense of responsibility for their neighbourhood.'

The idea of making them blossom out was actually successful; shouts and laughter ensued, interrupted every now and then by the blowing of a whistle. Taking advantage of the fact that my children were behaving like little angels – it was siesta time and they and the two monitors were fast asleep – I went round to the other side. A young teacher from the Jesuit college introduced herself. Unfathomable eyes in a clean-shaven face gave him the look of a conquering Caesar. Indeed, it was soon quite obvious that he had conquered all those young people. It was 'Ostaz Fayez' here, 'Ostaz Fayez' there. Bears freshly modelled from clay in the twinkling of an eye, his skill at soccer, the way he managed to sort out the progress of their games – all won him admiration. For a month, joy permeated the eucalyptus, morning, noon and night.

'I would like those of our students who came to work in this district to get to know the ragpickers' shanty-towns,' Father B said to me. 'Try and take them there one evening.'

He was right, these young people who had been more or less spoiled by life needed to have a close look at some of its other realities.

Off we went together. One of them called Philip politely relieved me of my bag, which was always quite heavy. The idea was to sort out the particularly thorny question of registering children for school. Getting the parents' signature always presented a problem. – 'I don't know how to sign my name.'

'That doesn't matter,' insisted Philip, undeterred. 'Just spit on your thumb first. Good, there we are!' He solemnly administered dye to the finger and stuck it resolutely on the appropriate place. We got back at ten o'clock at night with everything happily accomplished.

Sister Ghislaine and I had been invited to a celebration which was to conclude a month of noisy enjoyment. It was time for statistics: 'Fayez, how many youngsters did you have?'

'A hundred, but only about twenty girls.' The outcome of the inquiry was always the same. When would we manage to liberate the women and girls?

The children were sitting under the thick branches of a huge sycamore tree. Its venerable trunk almost shook with the shrieks of joy that greeted us. What in the world could possibly be more harmonious than the cries of children? They are life itself breaking out in a chromatic scale.

The festivities went off relatively calmly. Little girls danced gracefully before the admiring eyes of the little boys. The girls had emphatically refused to play ring-a-ring o'roses with the boys: they wanted the two sexes to be kept rigorously apart. The game which created the most uproar was the one where three boys had to swallow a thread leading to a packet of biscuits as quickly as possible. The thread entered and exited from the three oral cavities to the

110

accompaniment of much agitation and shouting. In the end when the first one reached his goal hands clapped and feet danced for joy.

The moment for presenting the prizes had arrived; the most hard-working and the most capable came to pick out either a tiny car or a little plastic doll. Blessed are the poor, a fourpenny toy was their ticket to heaven.

There was general excitement until Nader, the young Jesuit student, in charge of the games, blew his whistle for silence. Father B was going to speak. He had a gift for making himself understood by all kinds of audiences. He explained to them that the primary reason for getting together had been to promote love and understanding between Christians and Muslims. The children listened solemnly. Some of them would be going to a camp where, wonder of all wonders, they would stay overnight. 'What was the purpose of all these activities?'

The youngsters thought about it. 'To teach us to stand on our own two feet.'

'Exactly, what else?'

'To get us ready for the army,' one urchin with melancholy eyes called out determinedly.

'Very good, yes, but what else?'

They couldn't think of anything else. 'All right then – to make you capable of running your neighbourhood yourselves.' The youngsters' mouths dropped open, they were flabbergasted by the new role that had been attributed to them.

They left, already feeling the weight of a man-sized load on their backs.

6. Encounters day by day

The tourists

The *Catholic International News-bulletin*, a magazine which I particularly appreciate for its insight into world affairs, organized a trip to Egypt and I had the opportunity to meet those involved. Here is a letter I wrote to them:

> It was only yesterday that we said goodbye as you left ancient and modern Egypt to rediscover what is dear to you in France and elsewhere. Let me first congratulate you. You didn't come here simply as tourists curious to see exotic sights but as people wanting to get to know other people, a fact which was symbolized in one very simple gesture – the hands that some of the group held out to a taxi-driver who had risked his car on a poor road to save them tiring themselves out walking. This gesture was a concrete response to the hymn we sang at morning mass, 'hands outstretched to you, Oh Lord . . .' to grasp those of our brothers, too.
>
> You also managed to organize lectures on the country, which held people's interest despite the fatigue of bodies that had been trekking round town all day.
>
> I would like now to ask you a question: you came from a prosperous country to spend fourteen days in a country still in the throes of its development. By the time you read these lines you will be getting back into gear: have you changed at all? Yes or no? I would be amazed if you were still living in the midst of so luxurious a society in quite such a carefree fashion, in the knowledge that on the other side of the world more than a billion of your brothers are only just managing to keep body and soul together.
>
> You didn't appear to be the kind of tourists who focus their eyes on the camel rather than on the camel-driver, on the ancient four-thousand-year-old stones rather than on

112

the youngsters who would like to live as your children do. You were shocked, and I heard you talking about it: 'What can we do? How can we act on our convictions?' Raw materials supplied at a ridiculous price were a sore point – ranging from bananas and cocoa through to coconuts and cotton (not to mention petrol: that's far too 'inflammatory' a subject).

'I really do need my car,' some of you said. 'Oh, mine's only a mini, after all.' 'What aid organizations can we support?' – The tiny achievements of Catholic Aid: a well to water the fields, cattle to make up the number of livestock, equipment to build up a village and help it on its way? – And then what about the emigrants, isn't there plenty we could do in our own countries in Europe?'

It did me good to keep quiet and listen to you. I had just hurled plenty of invective at you about the poverty of some and the wealth of others. 'Let them gorge themselves with it until they burst, as Pascal used to say,' I announced quoting my literary sources. It wasn't very kind of me, considering you were there so receptive, so willing to understand and to share. You must excuse an old rag-picker who was looking straight through you at a nation too well provided for. The Bible compares the face of one who shares with the 'sun at midday', if you have taken some of its rays back with you from Egypt, you will set the world on fire with it. Congratulations in advance!

The student who risked his life

It was Saturday. Sister Ghislaine was expecting me in town at two o'clock, but it isn't always easy for me to get away. Samia arrived: 'Ableti, will you have a look at my knee?' With the dressing done, I started out but hadn't gone more than two steps when Mahmoud called out to me from down the street: 'Ableti, Ableti!' I turned back. He was bringing his little sister, with a cut in her arm, full of pus. On with the ichthyol ointment and I set off again, walking quickly. Then Om Samir called out from her doorway: 'Come and have a look at Samir.' The child was burning up with fever

113

and I was worried. 'Listen, Om Samir, I'm not a doctor. The child must see a doctor today – do you understand? – today.' She promised to take him to the neighbouring village.

By two o'clock I was almost at the station. The Cairo train was arriving and I made a dash to catch it. I had to cross the track. The Merg train was coming from the opposite direction but there was just time for me to get across when – whoops! my foot caught and I fell over in the middle of the rails. The engine was coming on at top speed, but dazed by my fall, I couldn't manage to get up. Suddenly I felt myself being grabbed by the shoulders and dragged off the rails, just as the train passed by beside me.

Sister Ghislaine was expecting me at two o'clock. With a gasped thank you to my rescuer I leapt aboard the Cairo train. Gradually I came to my senses. Someone had been prepared to die for me and I had hardly looked at him, hardly thanked him. I was deeply ashamed. Whatever happened, I must find him again.

On the Monday, I questioned some of the people at the station: 'Were you there when I nearly went under the train?' – 'No . . .' 'No . . .' 'No . . .' At last someone answered, 'Ah yes, it was you!'

'Do you know the person who saved me?'

'No, but he must have been a student from the local teachers' training college.'

I went there and asked to see the principal. I explained what had happened.

'Saturday at two o'clock . . . the second years left early.' He sent someone to the class. A young man with honest eyes, an expressive face, straight shoulders, and generally likeable air came in.

'Yes, when I saw you on the rails, I remembered my father's words, "Your first duty is to help others",' he said simply.

'What's your name?'

'Mohamed Fauzy.'

I shook his hand warmly and the teachers

applauded. He went out with the same air of simplicity. What could I give him? A real pen with a nib, that's what most of our less fortunate pupils dreamed of.

The following week, as I gave Mohamed this simple little present I said to him: 'I'd like to meet your father . . . and your mother.' He was thrilled at the idea. We arranged to meet on the Saturday. Together, we arrived at a very small flat. 'I haven't said anything to my parents, you know. When you do good, you should keep quiet about it,' he warned me before we went in.

I found myself shaking hands with a plump, kindly man whose face radiated goodness. I congratulated him on his son. 'He didn't do anything exceptional,' he answered. 'We are all God's children, so we should all help each other.'

Jesus was speaking through the mouth of this Muslim.

Bread and salt

The holidays arrived. I knew that, like most of the other students, my young rescuer, Mohamed Fauzy, wanted to learn to speak English perfectly. So I went to his house to suggest that he used his holidays to take lessons in town.

'Have you eaten?' asked his mother.

'Oh, I've already had a bean sandwich.'

'You must have something to eat with my husband.' On a small round table she set out a simple meal: aubergines with tomatoes, raw onions, lettuce leaves. It was three o'clock. She wouldn't be eating anything, she explained, because she had already had her meal, but she brought in some salt. She took a piece of bread, dipped it in the salt and put it in her mouth. 'Now we are friends for ever,' she said with a smile. 'We have shared bread and salt.'

I couldn't help thinking of the book of this title by

Père de Beaurecueil who says that from Afghanistan to Egypt the sharing of the food of the poor is like a sacrament—love springs from it. Differences of race or creed disappear, brothers sit side by side in a new communion. Père de Beaurecueil affirms that there too Christ is present.

My young friend, Mohamed, was delighted to be able to take English lessons. I went into town to register him. At the end of the holidays, I saw him again. He looked tired.

'Well, Mohamed, how did it go? Do you speak English well now?' I asked in English.

'I hardly started the course,' he replied sadly.

'Have you been ill?'

'Not me, my father. He could only work part time.'

'So, what did you do?'

'I took a job coaching primary school pupils who had exams to resit.'

'All day long?'

'Yes, there were two lots—one came in the morning, the other in the evening. I didn't have any time left.'

'You seem very tired, Mohamed.'

'Yes,' he smiled, but it meant that my father could get some rest.'

Sharing bread and salt with this family, is truly a *baraka*.

The disobedient daughter

Every now and then some delightful young girls come from Cairo to spend a morning or an afternoon with the ragpickers. The children are delighted to have an older friend to sit with them and help them to read or hem their knickers. One of these dedicated helpers would sometimes talk to me quite openly about her escapades. She came from a very restrictive background and from time to time out of sheer defiance she would secretly let some young stranger take her out.

'We go to the Pyramids and he'll buy me a coca-cola. There's nothing wrong with that!'

'Obviously not, but . . .'

We had had several long talks in which I tried to explain the facts of life to this girl who was so fresh and innocent.

One day her mother arrived, looking quite distracted: 'Is my daughter here?'

'No, I haven't seen her for quite some time.'

'She didn't come home last night.'

I trembled for my young friend. The story spread rapidly amongst the ragpickers. 'If she does come back, her father will kill her,' Labib told me. 'Honour has to be avenged!'

She arrived home a week later like an injured bird. It wasn't to the Pyramids that she had been invited this time; she had been shut up in a house with boarded-up windows. Her father didn't kill her. He had abandoned the customs of Upper Egypt, commented Labib.

One day one of my little girls told me a story about her sister. At that time they had been living not far from Assiout in Upper Egypt. The village was made up mainly of Christians but there were also a few Muslim families. One day their father, Deif, discovered that his eldest daughter had been seen chatting with a certain Mohamed. He stood her in front of him: 'Is this true?'

'Yes,' replied the young girl bravely, 'I love him, we want to get married.'

His only answer was to seize a horsewhip and shower her with blows, until she fell down spattered with blood. Then he kicked her. 'That'll teach you to love a Muslim, you bitch.'

But this modern Juliet was indomitable – she still managed to see her Romeo-Mohamed every now and then. No one was going to stop her marrying him. One evening her uncles came to confer with her father. The honour of the family was at stake. If she wouldn't give in, she would have to be killed. Deif agreed. The three of them would do it together; divided between the

117

three, the prison sentence would not be so heavy for any of them.

The first hours of the night passed slowly as the three men sat on the ground outside the door. In the little mud-walled house everyone was asleep. They crept up on Noura menacingly: 'Do you swear to give him up for ever?' they demanded in low voices.

'No.'

'You will die.'

She knew, but she preferred death to life without Mohamed.

They threw a cover over her head to suffocate her.

'Will you give him up?'

'No,' came the stifled gasp.

They stuffed the cover into her mouth: 'Will you give him up?'

'No,' she shook her head feebly.

They waited a few moments then the six hands loosened their grip. There she lay lifeless. Her name was Noura – Light. The light had been extinguished, but their honour had been saved.

After Deif came out of prison, I saw him several times. When his wife gave birth to a son, he held the child in his arms so delicately, you would have thought him the very gentlest of men.

The prison wives

Every now and then I pass the police station and every time I do, I see women dressed in the customary full black *melaya* (a kind of very ample veil which covers them completely) sitting on the pavement opposite. The faces change, but the anxious look directed at the door of the police station is always the same. Often they have one baby clinging to their breast and another hanging on to their skirt.

I discovered the solution to this mystery the day the police van arrived just as I was passing. The unfortunate women were waiting there with bated breath:

would their husband, father or son be thrown in it to be taken far away to prison or would he be released? A line of police officers was there to prevent any contact with the prisoners, but sometimes a woman would manage to sneak over to the vehicle for one last look, one final word. When the van started up, the women got to their feet silently, pulled the *melaya* back over their faces and disappeared.

Not far from the police station, there is a magnificent villa with a garden. Its walls had been newly repainted and its entrance renovated to bring it up to date. 'It belongs to a multi-millionaire,' it was explained to me.

'Is he in a good line of business? – in cotton?'

'Cotton, my foot! He's a hashish trafficker.'

'But that's against the law.'

'Of course it is, that's why it pays. He hands out bribes right, left and centre, he has friends in high places. He can't be touched. The petty middle-men are rounded up and stuck in prison while he runs about in a Mercedes, and travels abroad.

It's the same old story in every country in the world. A few fat fellows lead a life of ease on their ill-gotten millions while other poor fools get themselves put in prison.

The day of reckoning will eventually come. The book of Revelation shows us the sudden fall of Babylon the great and its whining traders: 'Alas, alas, for you, great city . . . decked with gold, and precious stones and pearls, your riches are all destroyed within a single hour.'

And even if your opulence should last for ever, oh Babylon the great, there are still people on this planet who prefer the hovels of Harlem and the Algerian slums of Paris to the skyscrapers of New York and the palatial buildings of the Champs-Elysées. There are still people who do not hesitate to risk prison and torture to help others.

Two thousand five hundred years ago Plato asserted coolly that 'the righteous man is happier in the cauldron of burning bronze than the tyrant who casts him into it'. Obviously he wasn't speaking from personal experience, but all the same he deserves our thanks for the insight.

The Bedouin women

An experience some years earlier, of life among the Bedouins of Egypt, provided me with a kind of introduction to the life of the ragpickers, particularly the women.

Some forty kilometres from Alexandria the oasis of Mariout forms a patch of green in the middle of the sands. In the desert not far from the villas which lie scattered among the palm trees, the Bedouins set up their tents. Together with a group of Sisters from our school in Alexandria, I went there for a few days' rest in a lovely house lent to us by friends.

The contrast between our comfortable life with its water, electricity, pleasant surroundings and varied diet, and theirs, which was devoid of all these things, was intolerable. It was all too easy to say 'They're used to it.' Of course their women would prefer to turn on a tap rather than have to go and fetch water from some distant spring, carrying a can on their heads. Who wouldn't jump at the chance to exchange paraffin for electricity and the pan under the bed for a refrigerator? Inside their tents some of the girls wove carpets in an artistic variety of colours, out of wool from their goats, but most of them were idle and knew nothing.

I thought I'd put the rest of the holiday to good use. Instead of going back to Alexandria I would try, together with some of my former pupils, to teach them to sew and write a little. People did their best to dissuade me: 'They're all thieves, dirty, ignorant and what's more they're quite happy to live in dirt and ignorance.' There was encouragement for you! But even as I listened to their gloomy pronouncements, I asked myself why, if man was so contented with his primitive lot, we weren't still in caves, dressed in animal skins.

We began by visiting the tents. We sat on the ground, every now and then we drank a glass of tea, and we became friends. The girls were thrilled at the prospect of coming to learn something but we had to be careful that they weren't of a marriageable age; after the age of twelve or thirteen, they were absolutely forbidden to leave their tents, except to go and fetch water.

The day for the first lesson arrived and the teachers were as excited as the pupils, whose good will was quite touching. We were going to start by making knickers which would be theirs to keep when they had finished them. If they were capable enough they would make a dress and then embroider a handkerchief. The schedule was tight because they were also to learn how to write their names, and every day there would be a short lesson in morality, and in first aid practice within the limited available means.

Often our Bedouins would run out of patience and throw their unprotesting knickers in the face of their young teacher. 'I've had enough, I'm going!'

I was summoned: 'Will you come over here Sister, Mabrouka wants to leave.'

I looked at the hem. 'But it's not that bad, Mabrouka, in a few days' time you'll be quite adept. Wait, I'll help you press on a bit.'

She smiled and sat down again.

When the time came to make themselves a dress, they were ecstatic. They needed quite a lot of help to finish them but in the end we got there; we couldn't leave before they had all tried on their handiwork.

Morality was another thing that captured their interest — starting with very concrete precepts: 'Who created the palm tree?'

'*Rabbuna*, the Lord,' they chorused.

'He also created the camel,' called out Mabrouka.

'And the chickens and the goats,' added Zayneb.

They got as far as the stars, together with the sun and

the moon. With that sense of the transcendent nature of God possessed by all those who live in the desert, our Bedouins marvelled at the beauty of all creation and thanked the Lord for it.

They were charmingly spontaneous. No, it was wrong to lie. Fatma was a great liar to the extent that nobody believed her any more, so what did she gain by it? It was not good to steal your neighbour's eggs. Why? We sought an answer together. 'Because God is just,' exclaimed Fatma, 'so he doesn't want us to be thieves.'

What if you had a bad stomach-ache? You poured some sand, burning hot from the sun, into a bag and put it on your stomach. This simple procedure delighted them. What about sore eyes? You took a clean cloth, dipped it in tea with no sugar in it, and there you had a good compress for your eyes. And for diarrhoea? The cooking water from the beans they ate daily.

They all wanted us to visit their tents, so we used the afternoon medicine round as an opportunity to call on them. With drops for their eyes, aspirin for fevers, mercurochrome or black ointment for their numerous wounds, so quickly infected by the flies — we were called from one tent to the next.

When we reached Zeynab's father's tent he was sitting on his mat, intoning the Koran. We waited until he had finished, then he told us with some satisfaction that he was a hundred and twenty years old: 'I was born in this tent in the time of Said Pasha. Mariout was just desert. I populated it with my children and my grandchildren.'

'How many children do you have?'

'Oh, I don't know. I've been married about fifteen times,' he added simply. (I have heard it said that he took it in turns to either bury his wives or send them back where they came from.) 'The last one I married is Zeyneb's mother.' How could that little desert flower, the most intelligent and the prettiest of them all, possibly be the daughter of this tyrannical centenarian? Zeyneb explained that, if anyone switched their radio to any other station but the Koran, her father would throw it on the ground and smash it.

When we returned a few months later, Zeyneb was about to get married. She was thirteen: the bridegroom was fifteen, but she seemed to be the one in control. 'I don't want to live in a tent,' she informed him. 'You'll have to make us a proper little house. I'm beginning to know how to sew. Buy me a machine and I'll make the local dresses. I shall earn some money to furnish the house.'

The girl who worried me most was poor Mabrouka. In an attempt to understand why she was so unstable, we went to see her at home. There, all became clear. We found ourselves confronted by a young woman who seemed difficult to get on with. She was Mabrouka's stepmother; her mother had been sent home by her father and the girl had been kept to wait on his new wife.

When I went to live with the Cairo ragpickers, of course, I had to leave the Bedouins of Mariout but they were lucky enough to have Sister O of the Sisters of Charity, take charge of them. Passing through Alexandria again one day, I went to visit them and Sister O showed me countless marvels produced by these desert girls: drawings, pieces of embroidery, bags, and so on. Each had followed her own inspiration. My eyes fell on an object which had a particular charm about it. On it I read the name, Mabrouka.

'What, our madcap Mabrouka?'

'Oh yes, that's the one.' Sister O explained that she had let the girls work with clay quite a lot. This kind of work provided Mabrouka with an outlet for her frustrations. She had fallen in love with it and gradually her fine artistic talent had come to light.

'Those Sisters of Saint Vincent may have had their successes,' I said to myself, 'but whenever someone comes to me to complain about her stepmother I shall give her this tip: Take it out on some clay and, who knows, you might come up with a masterpiece!'

The philosopher

I first met Mme Hatinguais a very long time ago. I was based in Turkey, and about to leave for Paris to see my family again for the first time in many years, but I also wanted to take the opportunity of bringing myself up to date on educational matters – everything changes, even the good old Sorbonne!

'You'll find the very best of Paris at Sèvres,' someone advised me, 'at the experimental high school and the International Centre for Pedagogical Studies, founded by the incomparable Mme Hatinguais.'

As soon as I entered Mme Hatinguais' office, I met with a smile and a light. Everything about her was welcoming, from the shining eyes, transparent as spring water, to the lips parted in a radiant smile. I had gone to meet a stranger; I found myself with a friend.

She immediately made me put myself down for a session for teachers of French to foreigners. I attended a sample lesson by Mme Stoudzé on *The Little Prince*. It went off like fireworks. She seemed to juggle with the simplest expressions, of the kind accessible to foreigners, and make them explode into flashes of thought. Mme Hatinguais spoke next on the theme of how to educate, *ex-ducere*, bring out the hidden riches in a child. I felt as if I was listening to Socrates and his dialectic. Yet, intellectual that she was, she was still not bogged down in abstractions: some pupils who seemed to have little talent for study would suddenly turn out to be fine artists. She would take us to see some of their work. But to bring forth life, we must first love:

We in the world must love each other
For as long as we live we must love.

The words of Paul Fort resounded on her lips. She delivered them with such vibrant joy that they seemed to envelop us completely.

What a week of enrichment! The lobes of my brain which had dried out during some of their convolutions in far distant countries (whatever would my teacher of cerebral anatomy say to that!) were suddenly refreshed. I left, rejuvenated in heart and spirit. Every now and then I would send Mme Hatinguais a letter telling her about the achievements of my pupils, or the efforts being made among the Bedouins. She was particularly interested in the awakening of those desert girls. In response, she would send me words of encouragement, always so heartfelt, about the progress of the ragpickers.

One day a large white envelope arrived for me, containing the announcement of the death of Mme Hatinguais. On the first page was a vase of flowers, with, underneath it, a passage from the prophet, Jeremiah: 'I see a rod of an almond tree . . . the tree that watches and waits . . . and is the first to wake; in the same way God watches over you and God is love.' I sensed her presence beside me just as if she were still alive, saying: 'Sister, you must love, love with your very last breath.'

'Yes,' I replied, 'as you did, Mme Hatinguais.'

And since that day, it's as if every now and then she visits the little room where the ragpickers, young and old, practise their reading and writing, because 'Love endureth beyond the grave'. It was she who wove the deep bond of friendship between dear M. Hatinguais, his two daughters and me and my ragpickers.

Here's what her erudite daughter Jacqueline wrote to me: 'In the Latin language, where the vocabulary is often ambivalent, cento denotes a cover made out of bits and pieces skilfully patched together; this kind of cover, impregnated with water, being the favourite adjuvant of the Roman firemen, the centonarius could be either a ragpicker or a fireman or both. So you see how the term, centonarius could augur well for the leaders in your work.'

Knowing one's literature has its uses: in the absence of firemen in our shanty-town, I could arm myself with a patchwork *cento* made out of old bits of cloth (a speciality of ours) and then if a fire were to break out anywhere I could rush round with it . . . and my rag-pickers could do the same. We could form a body of experts and offer our services wherever fire-engines were as yet non-existent!

But that wasn't all! 'Has it ever occurred to you,' added Jacqueline, 'that the Latin term for the most intense form of examination – which is ultimately metaphysical – is the verb *scrutari*, which originally meant "to forage amongst the garbage" and which, ennobled by Seneca, ended up meaning: "to fathom the unknowable" . . . or such disconcertingly change-able entities as the human consciousness.'

Yā salāam! To my shame I had to admit that my poor little brain had never conceived such profound thoughts, but really it does make you stop and think. Bent over his garbage, Seneca had been led to 'fathom the unknowable depths of human consciousness'. Those Romans were realists after all.

So, come on now, Seneca, tell us – the ragpickers and I, who live among the garbage heaps, are we human in the fullest sense? O philosophy! Wherever might you lead us?

The sisters

The bus was taking me to a town where, I had been told, there was a community of a new order of Coptic Orthodox nuns. It dropped me off at a busy market where men and women were filling their baskets with oranges, bananas and dates still hanging in bunches on their yellow stems. As always in Egypt, there was someone eager to show me the way to the *motraneya*, the residence of the bishop who had founded the community. The convent, marked by rousing singing, a light blue flight of steps and a wide open door, stood

126

opposite. A kindly Frenchman greeted me: 'Good day Sister, how nice it is to see you.'

'Did you get my card?'

'No, but there's a room ready and waiting for you.' With a smile *Tassouny* (Sister) Tahany led me away. She stopped to make a low bow before the iconostasis in the little chapel, then opened a newly painted door. There was just room for a bed, a wardrobe and a table in front of the wide open window: icons in fresh colours hung on the walls. On the table were a Bible and some devotional books: 'Make yourself at home. In half an hour we shall be saying our breviary and afterwards we shall have something to eat.'

During the next fortnight, this little convent, so bright and cheerful, was to show me a world I had never seen before. From morning till evening everything there resounded with hymns to *Yesou Habibi* (Jesus my Beloved). When I went past the kitchen a young novice was singing as she cleaned the aubergines. In the laundry room another one was singing as she vigorously washed the linen. With her skirts tucked up, Tassouny Tahany, the young Sister Superior, tipped a bucket of water over the steps and sang as she scrubbed. Soon the sound of a cymbal announced that it was time for Sext. Barefoot as we entered the sanctuary, we squatted on our haunches in the chapel: psalms followed one after another, interrupted only by intervals during which we prostrated ourselves to pray. Six times a day, those who weren't busy in the kindergarten, the workroom, the children's home, visiting the sick, and so on, would meet in this way to praise the Lord.

'It's Sunday tomorrow, would you like to come with us to a mass celebrated by *Sayedna* (the Lord Bishop)?'

'Can I take communion?'

'Of course.'

As the long Orthodox mass progressed the singing was interrupted by vigorous interjections of *Kyrie eleison – ya Rab irham!* from the people: The bishop had spotted me amongst the congregation. I saw him say something to Tassouny Sophie who came over to me and explained: 'Sayedna asks whether you would mind not taking your communion in front of the people, who wouldn't understand what a Catholic nun was doing. I'll take you to the Catholic church myself this evening so that you can take your communion. Tomorrow, Sayedna is coming to celebrate mass especially for us.' With veiled heads, the women went forward to first receive the consecrated bread, and then drink the consecrated wine from the golden spoon. Tassouny Sophie didn't take communion. 'I felt your anguish so deeply,' she told me later, 'that I prefered to share in your pain, because that too is a form of communion with the Lord.'

The following day the bishop came to celebrate mass at the convent. Afterwards he had breakfast with us and asked me with a smile whether I was happy.

'Well, yes, but not completely,' I said.

'Why's that?'

'Because I am waiting for the day when I shall be able to take my communion publicly in the Coptic Orthodox church.'

'We're getting there, but first we have to broaden a few minds.'

Twice he invited me to his table for a simple, frugal meal which all those who came to see him at that time were invited to share: Jerusalem artichoke soup with small pieces of meat, rice, courgettes in tomato, dates and oranges. The bishop served everybody first in an atmosphere of joyous simplicity. People joked and laughed, not unkindly, at my Arabic accent, but we also talked in English and French and we cleared the table together before going through to the reception room for the traditional Egyptian tea. The bishop explained to me that he had wanted to found a community dedicated to apostolic work as well as to prayer. This was something altogether new in the Orthodox Church, which had previously only included enclosed orders of contemplative nuns. Furthermore, like the Sisters of Charity in the seventeenth century, a person who did not belong to an enclosed order could not be called a *rahba* (nun). They could only be described as 'consecrated'. This difficulty had been surmounted in a practical way with a touch of humour, by the use of a term stemming from the language of the ancient Pharaohs: '*tassouny*' meaning 'sister'. The bishop asked me about our rules. He had sent two *tassouny* on a tour of Europe to various Catholic and Protestant convents and kept in close touch with our religious houses in Egypt.

On Friday afternoon, I was sitting in the cathedral tightly packed with people, on the right hand side reserved for women. First the bishop led in the singing of a hymn, beating time energetically in a rousing rhythm. Then there was a reading from the Epistle to the Corinthians and afterwards he asked some questions: 'Tell me the meaning of *takalit* – tradition.' Men and women of all ages, among them a number of young people, put up their hands, but no one could find a satisfactory answer. In the end, like a father talking to his children, he explained with a smile the two types of tradition: 'apostolic', which was common to all the Churches, and 'denominational', belonging to the different Churches in the world; he then indicated the bishop's throne, which he wasn't using because he preferred to walk up and down the centre aisle to be closer to the people. 'Do you see, that throne is traditional, but did *Mar Boulos* (St Paul) have one?' Everyone laughed. 'What matters is the teaching of Mar Boulos and not the *takalit* which subsequently developed differently in the different Churches.'

The next time I saw him, I told him how delighted I was that he was preparing his people for union with the Catholic Church on the basis of a common belief in the apostolic tradition. Of all the Orthodox Churches it is the Coptic Church which, despite all obstacles, is making the most rapid progress towards constructive dialogue.

In the evening, back in my little room, after singing psalms and sharing cheese and dates with the *tassouny*, I slept, or at least so I hope, the sleep of the just; at any rate I fell asleep with a happy heart. Often I was woken by the sound of a hymn being sung beneath my window in a stentorian voice. Intrigued by this nocturnal chorister, one morning I asked what the explanation was.

'Ah, our chorister,' *Tassouny* laughed, 'He's our convert to Christianity.'

'How's that? It doesn't happen all that often!'

'One day, he turned up saying he was suddenly convinced that Jesus was the *Mesih* (Messiah), *Ibn Allâh* (the Son of God), and that he wanted to become a *Mesihi* (Christian) too. He was baptized, obviously against the wishes of all his own people who showered him with abuse and blows. One day, they even dragged him off to the police station to accuse him of some crime and have him put in prison. Badly beaten and mocked, he only got out by virtue of the vigorous interventions of the bishop, who easily proved his innocence. He arrived here with his body battered but his soul elated. "How you have suffered my poor friend!" we sympathized, and bursting with joy this simple man answered "Oh I was happy to suffer for my beloved Jesus. Didn't he suffer more for me?"'

You, who are reading this, do you ever feel just a little lost in a modern world devoid of sanctity? If you do, just come to this little Coptic Orthodox community and bask in the joy of the gospel.

The woman who could forgive

One Saturday evening I had just arrived back at the house in Matareya when Marie came looking for me: 'Sister, come and persuade Samira to make it up with her mother. Perhaps she'll listen to you.' I followed her to the tiny flat where she lives – a small apartment with one room and a reception area.

'Good evening, Samira. How are you?'

'Very well.'

'Aren't you speaking to your mother any more?' She was silent for a moment with embarrassment: 'It's my sister's fault,' she went on.

'Why?'

'She insisted on my mother buying her a forty pound bracelet.'

'And then?'

'And then my mother didn't have any money left. I asked her for twenty pounds for some bricks' (she was building a little house) 'and she refused me.'

'If it's your sister's fault, why are you angry with your mother?'

'In her fury, Samira insulted her mother so deeply that she responded in kind,' explained Marie.

'Yes, she said such things to me!' She repeated them angrily for my benefit.

I didn't know what they meant. Marie smiled: 'You don't understand Arabic insults, Sister.'

'I shall never set foot in my mother's house again, never!' Semira stormed.

Suddenly Marie had an idea: 'Would you agree to come to Sister's home?'

'Of course I would, she has a *baraka*.

'And if your mother were there?'

'No, then I wouldn't come,' Samira said obstinately.

There was nothing we could do, so off we went to see her mother. We found ourselves confronted by an honest woman who in her turn sadly repeated her daughter's insults, the meaning of which I didn't understand. They were so bad that Marie couldn't translate them for me.

'Look, would you like to come to my home?' I asked her.

'Yes.'

'And what if we can get your daughter to come?'

'She's my daughter. I love her,' she replied with tears in her eyes. So we set out for the convent.

The door was opened by Sister Ghislaine, who offered us refreshments. Marie went off to look for Samira and, contrary to all expectations, actually came back with her. The two women clung to each other, weeping. The mother left, leaning on her daughter's arm.

'Marie, how did you work such a miracle?' I asked.

She hesitated slightly, then told us: 'It's no secret, everyone round here knows about it.'

'About what?'

'The business with Samira.' Then she told us all about what she had had to put up with a few years ago from Samira. Her husband, who was a somewhat fickle man, had taken a fancy to the lively young woman who lived with her husband and children in the neighbouring apartment. It wasn't long before she fell into his arms. 'As for me, I was beaten more and more frequently, but I had to put up with it for the sake of the children. I prayed to the Virgin Mary to save my husband and one day, he came home and said to me: "I've just been to church, I've made my confession and I promise you I'll have nothing more to do with that woman." A month later he fell ill and died in hospital. Afterwards I forgave Samira, I looked after her children and helped her. Today I said to her: "Look, didn't I forgive you for that time with my husband? And you're not prepared to forgive your own mother?" She cried and came with me.'

The heart of a child

So Marie remained a widow with her children. She worked hard to bring them up but it was difficult. 'Mummy, we would like some mandarins,' her little ones said to her one winter's evening. At five piastres a kilo they weren't too expensive. With the money in

132

their hands they rushed out but came back a little while later empty-handed.

'Well, children, what's happened?'

'Oh, mummy, the poor woman and her children were shivering with cold so we let her have the money.'

'I've got three dresses,' said eleven-year-old Wafa. 'I shall give one of them away.'

'I've got two pairs of pyjamas,' said seven-year-old Marie-Cécile. 'I can give one pair away.' And they each pulled out from under the bed the little chest in which their things were kept.

'And I've got an orange,' said four-year-old Youssef.

The three children rushed out again with their gifts. Marie let them go. She knew her Gospel: Let those who have two garments share with those who have none.

Marie-Cécile came home every day from school at about four o'clock, starving. 'And yet,' her mother said to herself, 'I give her a thick sandwich to take with her.'

In the end it was Wafa who gave the game away: 'Mummy, Marie-Cécile sees the poor man on the corner and gives him her sandwich every day.'

'Oh yes, mummy, he's hungrier than I am.'

'Except you become as little children, you will not enter into the Kingdom of God,' said Christ. But, Lord, it's not easy to have a heart like Marie-Cécile's – life is hard and it makes us hard.

Lord, through the grace of our children, grant that each one of us may recapture the heart of a child.

The widow

Linda was a simple peasant woman left unprovided for, alone with four children.

'It's not easy being a widow,' she said when she came to see me. 'Everyone's out to get you and no one comes to your defence even in those neighbourhoods where you'd expect otherwise.'

'What about your friends, Linda?'

'My friends? They're the same. All of a sudden they turn into animals. The other day I had to go and see Ibrahim who helps me out with my form-filling. Do you know him?'

'Of course, he's one of the best, you can tell that by his face.'

'Yes, yes, just wait till I tell you. I went to his office. He was sitting on one side and I was on the other. I took the papers over to him but he hardly looked at them. Instead he fixed his eyes on me: suddenly he stood up and his face – well, it was just like an animal's!'

She suddenly took her face between her hands and gave it an impressively bestial expression, just to show me. ' "Mr Ibrahim," I said to him, "Don't do that, don't come any closer, God is watching you." '

"What about me? I'm a man, after all," he replied. I was frightened, very frightened. So I appealed to the Blessed Virgin: "Come quickly, quickly. I'm alone with this animal." And do you know, she rushed to my rescue. Just at that moment a child came in: "I need a notebook, Mr Ibrahim." It's true that he's generally very good, but I don't know whether he's good or not any more. All I know is that his face changed in front of that child and I ran out quickly. Incidents like that often happen to me but I always appeal to the Blessed Virgin and she saves me from all those animals.'

Her distraught face resumed its serenity.

One day she had come to do some sewing with another widow. 'Let's say the rosary,' I heard her suggest suddenly, and slowly as her feet turned the machine, her chapped lips repeated: 'Hail Mary, full of grace.' The room reverberated with the two sounds.

'While the goddess of Reason sat enthroned in Notre-Dame, Christianity was saved by the simple prayers whispered by the women of the poor,' wrote Pierre de La Gorce in his book on the French Revolution. For as long as you, and others like you, live, Linda, animals will be muzzled and the earth will not be without its God.

Stones and kisses

Sometimes it so happens that little Mohameds pick up stones and throw them at cassocks or habits. The main thing is not to be upset by it. One day three youngsters did it to me. I turned round and they made off as fast as their legs could carry them but I caught one of them and offered him a sweet. 'Why did you do that? Have I done you any harm? Here, there are two more sweets for your friends.'

I carried on but soon I heard feet running after me. The three youngsters caught up with me again, panting for breath: 'Listen, we're sorry, we didn't know what we were doing.' I smiled at them and gave them a hug. Since that day we have been friends.

In another place, some little chaps, no more than knee-high to a grasshopper, picked up pebbles to throw at me but then a little girl came rushing over to me, grabbed my hand and kissed it effusively. Wasn't that delightful?

If only we could teach our children to love, regardless of any differences of creed, nationality or skin-colour, and make them repeat after Antigone: 'I was made for love, not hatred.' If only all the children of the world would hold hands. On that day the world would become a paradise where all the stones were turned into kisses!

7. Death and life

Killed by his friends

(Desperately upset by what had happened, I penned these lines while they were still fired by the blood of Ba'azak, but even now I don't know that I could write them any more calmly.)

He was eighteen years old, his name was Ba'azak and they killed him. He only wanted to live but his three friends killed him. Why?

At the age of fifteen, he arrived among the ragpickers and with a 'Gee up, donkey,' off he went to collect the garbage. He was a good, honest lad, always ready to work and he was liked.

They killed you, Ba'azak... Why? You only wanted to live. How did it all start?

Five days ago, on 11 February, you came back tired from climbing all those innumerable flights of steps. That evening your three friends said to you: 'Yallah, we're going to the café.' Where else could you go for a little relaxation, Ba'azak? Your hovel, like all the others, was made out of rusted cans. It didn't even have a window. You used to sleep there with your three friends.

'Yallah, let's go.' You all sat down at a table, and drank methylated spirits. At six piastres a litre it was the cheapest drink.

'Yallah, the cards.' You played and you drank; the alcohol burned your throats and the cards burned your eyes. By midnight you were still playing. Much to your misfortune, Ba'azak, you won.

'Yallah, I've won. You owe me fifty piastres.'

'Fifty piastres!' That was two days' earnings on the carts. The lads trembled with rage. 'Never, you thief!' Insults rained down.

Watch out, Ba'azak! Alcohol makes people see red. But you wanted your money. Was it for your old father, or to buy more drink? No one will ever know. In the end they threw your change at you with hatred in their eyes but there were still ten piastres to come:

'*Yallah*, my ten piastres.'

'Never.'

The four friends staggered out of the café, shouting with rage, to go and flop down together in their hovel. Watch out, Ba'azak! Alchohol makes people see red. Don't go to sleep, whatever you do; don't go to sleep, Ba'azak. The paraffin lamp flickered and went out. Ba'azak fell asleep in the darkness. Out came the knife blades . . .

'*Yallah*, you won't be able to demand your ten piastres again.'

'No, you would never ever be able to demand your ten piastres again. The three friends, blood-stained and heavy with drink, fell asleep . . . Four bodies lay stretched out side by side.

At four o'clock, Om Karima, who employed the four friends, came to wake them: '*Yallah*, up you get and on to the carts!' With a paraffin lamp in her hand she stood in the doorway. Her feet felt sticky. She looked down: Ba'azak, his three friends, her feet — they were all red with blood.

'Ba'azak, Ba'azak!' There was no answer. The three friends were in a drunken sleep. Om Karima began to scream. The neighbours came running.

'Quick, a donkey . . . tell the police!'

'*Yallah*, you three friends, what have you done to Ba'azak?'

Yes, they killed him. Why? He only wanted to live. His three friends are in prison, possibly for fifteen or twenty years. When they come out they'll be old and past it. I can hear you, my honest reader, with your clear conscience, saying: 'They only got what they deserved.' That may well be true, but tell me who is ultimately responsible – his three friends, or the society which takes advantage of their labours but lets them live like animals who kill their own kind? That society is you, me, us. That's all well and good, I hear you say, but what can we do about it? What can you do? First take a look at the man who comes to collect your garbage. Look at him with the eyes of a brother: remember him in your prayers, in your thoughts; mention him to your friends sometimes. Who knows, perhaps then the Spirit of God who, St Paul tells us, is looking for 'helpers' to save men, will rouse some of them into tackling the problem of how to throw these people, particularly the young ones, a lifeline.

Yes, my three friends killed me, when I only wanted to live.

Could my death serve some constructive purpose?

Prison

The night of Ba'azak's senseless murder, I was in my little shanty and I can't help wondering to this very day how I didn't hear Om Karima's screams, because we don't live far from one another.

My alarm went off and up I got to go to mass. 'Hello,' I thought, 'my clock must be slow,' because it was already quite light when I came outside. My sisters don't like to think of me trotting across the fields alone at night. Personally, I'm not frightened but, to set their minds at rest, I borrow a little car from one of our neighbours. I jumped in and off I went to the station. On that tragic morning I can't have gone Om Karima's way. The police were conducting their investigations. No doubt they would have picked me up too, and asked me suspiciously what on earth I was doing 'out here in the middle of the night amongst this lot of assassins'.

Unfortunately, I missed out on this unhoped-for opportunity to go to prison. It's not all that easy, you know. I even wrote to the Governor General to ask for permission but he turned me down. I was for ever wondering what offence I could commit to get the chance to take those inside a little joy and hope.

One Easter day when I was still in Alexandria, I had gone with two of my little pupils and their mother to wish their father in prison a happy Easter. We stood in the street in the midst of a dense crowd. On the first floor some men were looking out from behind bars high up in the wall. We were determined to try to get in, despite all the obstructions. I forced a way through the crowds until an imposing police officer stopped me: '*Awza eh*? What do you want?'

'*El Nazer*, the Governor.' He took me instead to quite a young man, who seemed very pleasant.

'I have two children with me who want to give their father an Easter kiss.'

'*Mumken*, that's all right.'

'And I've brought the prisoners some oranges. May I hand them out myself?'

He hesitated slightly, but in the end he let me. He lent me a soldier to dig out my little girls and their mother and extract them from the crowd. While they waited in the yard I went off with an easy mind to see the women. With a smile, I offered each one an orange. The wretched things seized them with a long look of appreciation.

Suddenly, a soldier appeared beside me. 'Come with me,' he ordered me roughly. I followed him. He took me into the Governor's office. Looking imposing in his braid, he surveyed me with suspicion. I didn't want to appear to be too unnerved, so I asked for a chair and calmly sat down opposite him.

'What have you come here for?'

'To bring Easter greetings.'

'To whom?'

'Primarily to Guirguis Ezzat but also to the women.'

139

'Who is this Guirguis Ezzat?'

'The father of two of my young pupils.'

'What's he in for?'

'I don't know, his wife says he's innocent.'

He roared with laughter. 'The same old story, they're always innocent!' He gave orders to a police officer. We waited. The man came back, 'Yes, there is a prisoner called Guirguis Ezzat.' 'Yes, his two children are here, waiting to see him.'

'You see, I'm not a liar,' I said, looking him straight in the eye.

He was a bit put out. 'All right, I'll have this Guirguis brought out. You can see him in the yard, but you're not to see the women prisoners.'

'Why not? I wanted to give them these oranges.'

'It's against the rules. But leave the oranges here if you want, and I'll see that they get them.' He stood up and saluted me.

Shortly afterwards Guirguis was weeping as he hugged his children to him, when suddenly there was a movement in the crowd: two Orthodox priests in long black coats were forcing their way through with the help of some young men carrying cases. They had come to wish the prisoners a happy Easter. I longed to slip in behind them, but the braided Governor arrived, checked it all out and gave the curt order: 'The two priests only are to go through, *bess.*'

I still haven't been inside the prison. Who'll give me a tip on how to get myself locked up? All those unloved people are calling out to me from behind their bars, and I even managed to miss the opportunity to respond to them on the day that Ba'azak died.

The 30,000-dollar race

The day after Ba'azak's death, I turned up at the Jesuit college deeply depressed. 'Father M, please.'

He came in. 'How are you, Sister?'

'It's not working out.'

'Why not?'

'Because, can't you see, I'm not doing anything, you're not doing anything, we're not doing anything, and in the meantime our young people are killing each other.'

'Calm down, Sister, calm down. What's happened?'

Still very distraught, I told him the whole lamentable story. 'Ultimately it's all our fault, Father, mine and yours. If we don't build a youth club where our young people can spend their evenings in the pursuit of healthy pleasures, it'll happen again. They're not the murderers, we are!'

'You're exaggerating, Sister.'

'Not all that much, Father. Did you see that Cayatte film, "We are all Murderers" when it came out? I agree with him . . . Let's build them a hall.'

'We've already talked about it, especially over the last few months since the owner of the football ground reclaimed it.'

'Of course we have. Since that miserable day they haven't even been able to do their sport any more, and I've said to you time and time again: "Let's buy a piece of land!"'

'Yes, but you wanted to buy a field and build two kindergartens, a needlework room, a classroom for teaching the alphabet, a youth club, and you wanted to mark out a football ground all at the same time,' the priest replied, slightly annoyed. 'We worked out that all that came to 30,000 dollars. And on top of that, you've always said you wanted a swimming pool!'

I felt my blood boil. 'Let's forget about the swimming pool, Father, despite the fact that the ragpickers' need to cool off in summer is greater than most other people's. As for the 30,000 dollars, I shall go to Europe and get it. Find me some addresses and give me your blessing, and we'll move heaven and earth.'

The outcome of this conversation was that I was

equipped with the highest recommendations to bishops, nuncios, patriarchs. I sent them to various cities in Europe and off I went on my 30,000-dollar race.

The Egyptians

I've knocked about quite a bit in the countries of Europe, Asia Minor and North Africa – but nowhere have I found the people so friendly and courteous as in Egypt. Here's just one of innumerable examples.

I was getting ready for my quest for funds when I suddenly heard that as from April the reduced rate plane ticket was to be done away with. It would cost me another hundred pounds. There was just time to rush from office to office to conclude the formalities. Like my ragpicker friends, I only take a taxi as a very last resort but this time I had to get everything done before the offices closed.

I looked for a car and sure enough a taxi came along. But a lady in a hurry wanted to get in too. Ah! we were going in the same direction, we would both use it.

'Where exactly are you going, Sister?'

'To Swissair.'

'*Yallah yâ rais*, Swissair.'

'But what about you?'

'Oh that doesn't matter, I'll drop you off – it's only a slight detour – then I'll carry on. You look as if you're in more of a hurry than me.' She absolutely refused to let me pay my share and left me outside the agents.

Ever kind and courteous, Mr B had already sorted out my long, complicated journey. Three people were sitting in his office. 'Before leaving for Chicago via London, my wife would like to spend a few days in Switzerland,' a Lebanese gentleman explained. 'I'm going to join her the day before we leave.' While Mr B did his utmost to unravel this complicated

142

affair, I talked to two young people, a girl and a boy who were waiting. They were Egyptians going to spend their holidays in London. The subject of the ragpickers came up quite naturally in our conversation. It's one I know most about. The Lebanese went away satisfied and the two tickets to London were soon sorted out. Just as she was leaving, the young stranger slipped a large-denomination note into my hand: 'For your garbage people, Sister.' I didn't even have time to thank her. With a smile, she was gone.

'You're next, Sister. It was very difficult to find you a place on 31 March. Obviously everyone wants to leave on the last day of the cheap rates, but in the end there was one ticket left on Pakistan Airways so everything's in order. There's the bill for the whole lot, but give me ten pounds less. That'll be my contribution to your journey.' I left him, much moved by so much generosity and courtesy.

As I stood on the pavement, a car pulled up: 'Are you going to Zamalek, Sister?'

'Yes,'

'In that case, do get in.' I didn't have to be asked twice and we drove off. This charming young woman told me her name was Isis: a dream name, that of the moon goddess. When a red light brought us to a halt, a woman selling violets came rushing over and stupidly I exclaimed, 'Oh what pretty flowers.'

'Do you like violets, Sister?' she asked and without giving me time to reply, she bought a bunch and handed them to me. I thanked her, somewhat abashed. The car was filled with their subtle perfume. 'Whereabouts in Zamalek are you going, Sister?'

'To the nunciature.'

'Fine, I'll drop you there.' I left her, clutching my violets. Her name was Isis. That was all I knew . . . I would probably never see her again.

I went into the nunciature armed with fragrant flowers, an air ticket at a reduced price and ten pounds in my wallet. Mgr G had already written a personal letter of introduction to Rome. His Italian secretary, Father B, is a great friend of the ragpickers and their sister. He gave me detailed directions on how to get by in the city. ('*Urbs*', as our Latin teacher used to say, raising his voice with reverence. Just think, the city of Romulus and Remus!) I left, feeling very sure of myself. It was an auspicious day and I ought to mark it with a white stone as the ancients used to. There's no doubt about it, all the Egyptian moons put together couldn't grant such auspicious omens.

You really ought to come and see for yourself how people here put themselves out to do you a good turn. In the early days of my stay in Cairo, I had been to see the priest at Embaba and had to get back to Matareya. Was it far? A matter of one-and-a-half to two hours. I didn't know what means of transport to use. 'I'll accompany you as far as Matareya and then come back,' one married man with a family volunteered.

'Don't be ridiculous, that's absurd! Just put me on the first bus and tell me where to get off and where to catch the next one.' Believe me, I had to fight him off to stop him jumping on the bus with me. But then, what more could a woman want . . .

I could fill a whole book with tales of the kindness of so many Egyptian friends!

The blood of Ba'azak

All my documents were in order and I was thinking about Ba'azak. It was as if he were going with me. Yes, together we would save our young people.

My first place of attack was Rome where I telephoned 'The Church in Need'. 'Yes, Sister, we received your letter all right but Father Van Straeten, the director, is away. You come from Africa where we have numerous missions and not enough resources. You must understand our difficulties.'

144

'Yes, I do understand. If by some extraordinary chance, I am given more than the 30,000 dollars I need, I shall be able to help you.'

'Oh, thank you, Sister! Goodbye and good luck!' My first attempt had not proved very positive but not to worry!

My next telephone call was to Cardinal P. 'Oh yes, Sister, the nuncio told me about you,' said a pleasant but hurried voice, 'but I'm just finishing packing and then I leave for Paris. See Mgr B. Good luck, Sister!'

I found myself talking to a prelate with bright eyes and a precise way of speaking. 'Well, Sister, I have before me a file on the ragpickers. You want 30,000 dollars. That's quite a tidy sum. Have you started yet?'

'Yes, Bishop,' I told him very simply about my first attempt on the telephone.

'Look, Sister,' he concluded, 'if you carry on with those methods, you might as well go back to Cairo tomorrow. You won't raise anything. You worry about your ragpickers, Sister, not about all the other missions in Africa. And only use the telephone to make appointments. Use a little common sense, Sister!' Seeing my crestfallen face, he added: 'Come on, come on, I promised you a cheque to start you off. – Telephone "The Church in Need",' he instructed his secretary, 'and tell them Sister will be arriving. It's very near, over the bridge and turn right – the first house. Come back afterwards and pick up your cheque. Goodbye and here's to your success.'

I was really very fortunate to bump into that priest. Thanks to his advice, which I followed meticulously, I managed to open many a closed door. In the first place, I was given a charming welcome at 'The Church in Need'. A delightful girl called Antoinette listened to me with a generous heart. I told her the story of Ba'azak and all of a sudden I found myself quite ridiculously bursting into tears, something which only happens to me about once every ten years. I couldn't get over the death of that boy.

'Don't worry, Sister, we'll help you, that kind of tragedy will never happen again.'

I left feeling brighter, but why did the blood of Ba'azak seem to keep reappearing on my hands? They had never actually been dipped in it but sometimes I felt as if I could repeat with Lady Macbeth: 'All the perfumes of Arabia will not sweeten this little hand.'

Why do we have to have victims and bloodshed before we are prepared to go to the rescue of our brothers in need? One thing I can say is that the tragedy of Ba'azak never failed to raise help for his friends the ragpickers.

'What were you doing on 11 February this year at ten o'clock in the evening?' I would ask an apparently indiscreet question, and my astonished interlocutor would sometimes leaf through his diary and frequently reply: 'I must have been at home, Sister.'

'Tucked up in the warm with your electricity, your central heating and your television.'

'I never watch television, Sister,' some would go on to say.

'Perhaps not, but that apart, you were sitting down very comfortably after a good meal.'

'Like everyone else, Sister.'

'Like everyone else in your city, but at that time the only place four young twenty-year-olds had to spend the evening together was a hovel, three metres long by two metres wide, with flattened earth for a bed, no windows, no light, no water and no heating . . . and it was only a few degrees above zero. What else could they do but go to the pub on the corner?' I would carry on as dispassionately as possible. Then, with a lump in my throat, I would fall silent. On all the cheques I received, I seemed to see a few drops of blood.

Paris or Cairo?

I was in Paris, leaping on to the Métro. I had to go half-way across the capital city of my younger days to talk about the ragpickers. There was a seat – that was a godsend. I would be able to read my breviary quietly. I made the sign of the cross . . . then looked up. People were looking at me in amazement with a slight smile on the corner of their lips. Praying openly right in the middle of the Paris Métro, there was a really medieval nun for you! No doubt she would soon start mumbling her rosary too. And she was still wearing a habit! I wanted to smile back at them: 'Oh yes, ladies and gentlemen, just imagine, I come from a country where people pray openly in the streets and where a stranger once said to me: "Thank you! how nice it is to see a nun in a habit. It makes me think of Allâh!" '

In Cairo, when the muezzin's call rings out, the water-melon seller lays out his small, thin mat beside his cart, squats down on his haunches, bows his head till his forehead touches the ground and keeps it there prostrate for a few moments. *Allâh Akbar*, God is greatest. There is no god but God. Sometimes half the pavement is blocked for a few minutes with Muslims praying in this fashion; their eyes never stray from their deep contemplation of the Unseen.

How often I have joined with these souls at prayer on the suburban train from Cairo to the village near my ragpickers! While the man sitting next to me reads the Koran, I read psalms from my breviary. Both our prayers are human prayers and therefore imperfect but both censers send up a perfume which rises in a single spiral of praise to the Most High God.

He runs a rosary with thirty-three beads through his fingers, murmuring his way through it three times to glorify the Lord. The ninety-nine names for God are recited one after another: the Greatest, the

147

Best, the most Beautiful . . . While the Muslim's lips whisper the vocabulary of the Most Merciful, I go through the beads of my own rosary: 'Blessed art thou . . .'

When you're walking down the street, a truck will go by with the name of Allâh written on it in large letters. When you go into a large store, you'll find it again, hanging on the wall. Christians find a prominent place for their images of Christ or the Virgin Mary. When you go inside a house, the Koran or the Bible is laid out on the table in the small reception area. I am writing these lines during the month's fast for Ramadan. At more than 40°C the heat is stifling, yet millions of men, women and children will not drink so much as a mouthful of water from four o'clock in the morning till seven o'clock at night.

Is it tradition more than personal conviction? Fanaticism rather than the kind of religious belief that stems from the heart? Fasting that is better suited to laziness than to work? Fear of the All-powerful more than love for one's fellow men? There may be some truth in all these criticisms. Nevertheless (everyone to their own taste) I prefer the little suburban train of Cairo which slowly puff-puffs its way along carrying within its packed confines, amidst the unpleasant smells of crowded humanity, the incense of prayer, to the soulless Paris Métro.

The hold-up

'I must find those 30,000 dollars. If not I shall stage a hold-up,' I announced, somewhat carried away by my subject, during a conference held in Geneva.

There was a journalist present and the next day a Swiss newspaper carried the headlines in large letters: 'Nun ready to stage a hold-up.' Hmm. I forgot to follow that old and popular maxim, 'count ten before you speak!' Naturally I found plenty of young people ready to come to my assistance. 'They're getting the revolver ready, Sister.' I could already hear the whistle of bullets – Heavens, it was ominous! Come on now, put up your sword and be a good little inoffensive Sister!

I also scandalized some friends by admitting: 'Do you know, when I saw the Geneva supermarket overflowing with food for people, dogs and cats, I do believe that if I had been younger . . .'

'If you had been younger . . .?'

'I would have poured petrol over it and put a match to it.'

'Where would we be if even our nuns were to start lighting unlawful fires? There would be nothing for it but to fly to the moon!'

'You've got to understand that my transition from the ragpickers to the supermarket was too abrupt!'

The day I stopped off in Geneva again at the end of my travels, that usually peaceful town was in an uproar. What on earth was going on in Calvin's city? Streets were closed off, the place was crawling with policemen and police cars. Monsieur F, my friend Charlotte's admirable husband, turned on the television: 'For the first time in Genevan history there has been a hold-up at one of the large international banks. As you can see, the gangsters are inside.'

He turned towards me and with an expression of assumed anxiety said: 'I'm wondering if the police will come up here. During your last visit you solemnly announced in the newspaper that if you didn't get your 30,000 dollars you'd stage a hold-up. Now you turn up out of the blue, and look what happens!'

'Are you sure you haven't had something to do with it?' he inquired in the tone of a friend from whom no secrets can be hidden.

The Europeans

Here are some extracts from the letter I sent when I got back from my long journey.

My dear friends,

Having only just landed back among our dear ragpickers (I've written 'our' because you've adopted them too, haven't you?). I would first like to be with each one of you again in spirit . . . In my mind's eye, I can see all those friendly, sympathetic faces: you have all filled my heart with so much warm affection that I feel committed in my turn to extending it to our brothers the ragpickers, who are so unused to sympathy and regard!

There now, someone's ringing at my door! (I'm writing to you from the apartment in Matareya because, once I'm back in my shanty-town, there will be no peace to write) . . . it was Om Hamdi, whom you saw standing next to me in the photo. We embraced each other warmly. Just think, we hadn't seen each other for a month! We talked of you who have seen her and loved her and she left refreshed and happy.

1 April: I recall the first days of April spent in Rome where my greatest joy was an audience with the Pope; he looked pale and tired but his face was so radiant with goodness! . . . And what can I find to say about the Roman kindness, that of my Sisters on Janiculum hill, of the priests in the Vatican or those I met belonging to the various organizations and at dear San Vito! As for Brother Rodolfo's young pupils, I was astonished at the way they were so attentive and so unusually quiet for their age during the lecture I gave them.

5 April: With my purse already lined, I flew to Switzerland, where I thought people would be less expansive. Yet, piloted along by my dynamic Charlotte, I received such a warm welcome at the 'Terre

des Hommes', that you would have thought we had known each other all our lives. In Zurich I had the very great joy of meeting up with faces that I hadn't seen for forty years! I was given an amazing reception at the Protestant centre for Mutual Aid in Zurich and at the centre for Catholic Aid in Lucerne and the day before at the Ecumenical Council in Geneva. One soon feels a sense of fellowship with those who share the same ideals.

9 April: I had to fly off to London. A young Swiss helped to carry my luggage and sat next to me on the plane. 'We have a tremendous priest,' he confided. 'As we all live clustered around the church, he's given up his car and visits us on a bicycle. People bother him at all hours of the night and day but he never minds. He lives simply so that he can help the Italian colony. So in my family we all agreed to eat meat only twice a week and to give some to the new immigrants who have none. And if only you knew how beautiful our masses are!' He offered to show me round London, but a liveried chauffeur was waiting for me.

'Are you Sister Emanuelle?'

'Yes.'

Monseigneur H, our dear former nuncio, now in London, had sent for me. At his house, I told him about our Egyptian friends, and naturally about the ragpickers, in whom he took a very concrete interest. Then he had me driven to Cafod, an organization that took an interest in us and gave me the same delightful reception. Afterwards I was off to catch the train for Oxford. When I got off the train, a young student at the famous university offered quite spontaneously to take me to Oxfam. We chatted.

'In two years, I shall have finished my studies,' he told me.

'What job will you go after then, the one where you'll earn the most money?'

'Not on your life, the one where I'll be of most use

to humanity. I belong to an association of young people throughout the world, whose ideal is love for all men and the most effective service.' I listened to him, completely overwhelmed. Long live youth!

At Oxfam, I was received with open arms by the most charming person in the world, as Mme de Sévigné would say.

One night spent with our London sisters was enough to show me how dynamic they are. One of them had just left for Russia with a party of young people, another had gone to Palestine. A students' hostel, adjoining the home where the elderly sisters live, was bubbling with life. 'Don't ring the bell, Sister,' one charming boy called out to me. 'I have a key,' and he opened the street door. In England, things are progressive!

10 April: On to Brussels, the city where I was born, which would prove to be as generous as all the previous places. There I had wonderful reunions with very dear members of my family and former companions of my younger days. (Hello, there's a noise outside in the street at Matareya – cheering and a great to-do . . . When I went over to the window I could see women carrying baskets full of multi-coloured pieces of cloth on their heads: it was some young bride's trousseau, 'Inshallah! may she be happy!')

At my old school of the Sisters of Mary, I gave a talk to an audience that was particularly charming. Then I visited various organizations: Caritas, where I was listened to with the liveliest sympathy, the organization for pontifical works and 'Justice and Peace' where I found the same degree of interest. Belgium was pulsating with life. I took part in an unforgettable Easter vigil led by a young married deacon who had only recently been ordained: what life, what spirit, what a balance of ancient and modern liturgy! After mass I was invited to have a drink in the hall to celebrate the Resurrection of

Christ. It was full of young people singing and larking about! Long live youth!

17 April. I caught the train for Tournai . . .

I called on young families full of Christian vitality. The mother of three-and-a-half-year-old Viviane informed me that she had gone without chocolate for the whole of Lent for the ragpickers, 'Do the little ragpickers like chocolate?' Viviane asked me.

'Of course they do, Viviane, but it's too expensive for them.'

'And if I give them my chocolate?'

'Oh, they'll say: isn't Viviane's chocolate lovely!'

She laughed, showing all her dimples. At three-and-a-half, she had already learnt how to deprive her own mouth of chocolate to put it into the mouths of those who had none! Carry on like that, Viviane, and you'll go far.

20 April: Luxair took me to Luxemburg, where I made the acquaintance of a delightful little girl called Emmanuelle, aged six less ten days, as she told me with precision. She walked me solemnly through the streets and then showed me the lions and panthers in her miniature zoo. We became great friends and resolved to write to each other. The bishop received me with no less interest, and he too resolved to help us. It was certainly worth the effort of going to Luxemburg.

21 April: A lightning visit to Arlon to a young, lively and joyful community where I had a heated discussion with one of the most likeable Jesuits I have ever met . . .

'You'd have to hand out a million per head if you really wanted to build anything out of it, Sister.'

'Belgium is too expensive, Father.'

'We're not ragpickers, Sister!'

'More's the pity, Father. If Christ were to come again, he would live among the ragpickers.'

'You can't be sure of that.'

'At least it's probable, Father.'

23 April: Paris, the city of light! A quick stay, but one which was enriching in every respect. Visits and lectures followed one after another; the young and the not so young, religious and lay people, family and friends invited me to be their guest, questioned me and showed great interest. The young people from the Paris Zionists were fired with enthusiasm: 'Egypt is beautiful, the ragpickers are great, we'll come over . . .'

'Of course, I'll expect you.' I arranged for us to meet at the foot of the Sphinx. 'Write and let me know the date and the time. Come in a group. I don't have too much time.'

'All right.' . . .

27 April: Gave a talk at the school at Grandbourg and had the pleasure of speaking for one last time to young people who listened so eagerly and who proved to be as generous there as they had been everywhere else. One pupil emptied out her purse altogether. I was bombarded with questions. Oh how wonderful the young are: if our old civilization is decadent, it is they who will save it. . . .

28 April: I had two days left to slip over to Marseilles and Nice to see some of our dear Sisters . . . Then I had to set off once more to speed along the Côte d'Azur to Nice airport. We have even more beautiful beaches in Egypt where a fantastically blue sea washes vast expanses of golden sand. But wouldn't tourism spoil our people, who are so simple and wholesome, as yet uncorrupted by wealth and all its dubious pleasures?

30 April: Did the final lap to Geneva where so many gifts had accumulated, and paid a last visit to a kind and generous banker.

1 May: I landed at last in the good city of Cairo to be back among the dear people of Matareya: no more parking problems! I shall resume my beautiful simple life of sharing with the poorest of the poor, but it has gained something new: bonds of fellowship have

been formed. It is thanks to this very fellowship, which provided us with mountains not of snow but of dollars, that a dispensary and classrooms will soon stand on a clean, healthy piece of land; here the little ones from the kindergarten will come to frolic, here the girls will learn to sew and read, the boys and men will come to learn their alphabet and, best of all, our young men will get some exercise on the football pitch. Then at night the youth club will come to life with drama productions, recreational and educational films, laughter and song.

Thank you to each one of you for having brought to fruition the wish of the venerable Mgr Cayer: 'Help them to become men . . . then they will become sons of God!'

Thank you for all your tokens of interest and affection; the ragpickers and their Sister send you their love with the sign of Akhenaten: 'The gentle caress of the Egyptian sun as it shines in the morning and the evening.'

Samir, the little blind boy

I took with me to Switzerland a file on Samir, the little blind boy. Here's how I came to know him.

The Protestant Church in Cairo is wonderfully well-equipped with audio-visual material. Every now and then they send me their car fitted out with a battery and a film projector. Amin, who is one of the kindest of men, comes with it to keep an eye on the equipment.

One morning, just as I was jumping on the train, someone greeted me warmly: 'Ezayyek, How are you?'

'Hamdu li-lláh, Praise be to God!' He presented me with a ticket. It was Amin. I was touched, because he's by no means a millionaire. I looked at him now in broad daylight: in the field at night I had never noticed the sadness which veiled his face.

155

'Are you ill, Amin?'

'No.'

'Is there something wrong?'

'My little son, Samir, is blind.'

There can be nothing more moving than the mention of a blind child. It's always as if we grown-ups more or less deserve what befalls us, but little children who have not yet done anything wrong, shouldn't have to suffer.

'At the age of six, Samir saw his little sister die,' his father explained with tears welling from under his eyelids. 'About a fortnight later, he got up one morning and staggered about with his arms outstretched in front of him. "What are you up to, Samir," I asked him. "I can't see any more, daddy." We've tried all the doctors and all the hospitals with no results.'

I was due to leave for Switzerland in a few days. 'Put together a comprehensive file for me and I'll show it to "Terre des Hommes". Obviously I can't promise anything but we must try everything.'

A few days later, Samir arrived, led by his father, and accompanied by his mother and little sister. The child's large, brown, staring eyes were pure and beautiful like a still, clear lake. Just to look at him was enough to make you cry. I took the file. As they got up to go, Amin made a sign to his wife who, dressed in a faded but clean yellow dress, took out of her basket . . . a duck. 'We killed it for you yesterday. Just you see how good it is!'

Poor people! They had been fattening the bird up to savour it at Easter, and now they were going without it for me; but I would have hurt them too deeply if I'd refused it.

I arrived in Switzerland at Charlotte F's home. Ever ready to help anybody, she took charge of the file. I was back in Cairo when a letter arrived from 'Terre des Hommes' in Lausanne. The specialist didn't hold out much hope but he asked for another examination by an ophthalmologist. We went to the doctor. He scrutinized Samir's eyes meticulously. It was a tragic moment when he wrote his report: 'The optic nerve is no longer red, hardly even pink, more a whitish colour: there is hardly any hope.'

'There is no point in sending us the child,' Lausanne informed us.

I had to pass on the terrible verdict to Amin. We both had to hold back the tears. He had sold his little house and got himself up to his ears in debt in order to have Samir treated by all the local doctors, but it had all been in vain. Now his last hope had been shattered. Even the Institute for the Blind had rejected his child because his intelligence quotient was below the requisite level. If I could find the resources, I would try to send a teacher capable of developing him as much as possible, to visit his house. But would that be practicable?

With Amin there in front of me, a picture of despair, an idea came to me: 'On Saturday evening I'm free. I'd like to come and visit you all.'

Suddenly a ray of hope shone in his eyes. For these faithful people, anyone consecrated to God, brings with her the Lord's blessing. 'Rabbuna kêbir, Rabbuna maougud, The Lord is generous, the Lord is with us,' he said, less dejected as he shook my hand.

Samir likes to pray. When he does so, an indefinable joy washes over him. Who knows what brilliant dawn his dead eyes perceive? It is often said that the child and the old man live on the same mountain top.

There was one old ragpicker who used to sit out in the street, paralysed and blind. Whenever he was asked: 'Old man, what are you doing there? Aren't you bored?' he would look up at you with a face that was emaciated but radiant with a mysterious light.

'No, my daughter, I am never bored, I am giving thanks to God.'

'For what, old man?'

157

'I am giving thanks to God for the ray of sunshine that is caressing me, for the bird that I can hear singing in the distance, for the hen that has just laid an egg, and for the blue sky that others can see. I live joyfully, *hamdu li-llâh*, praise be to God! He is very close to me.'

When it comes down to it, which of us is really blind?

Forgive those who killed me

A shaft of love can shine through even blood and tears. The following letter was written by Ghassibé Kayrouth, a twenty-two-year-old student preparing for ordination at the Jesuit college in Jamhou near Beirut. He left there on 20 December 1975 to spend Christmas with his family in his home village of Nabha where Maronite Christians and Metouali Muslims live side by side. On the way there he was murdered near the ruins at Baalbeck. When he set out he left an envelope in his room marked: 'From Ghassibé,' and containing this testament in Arabic:

'In the name of the Father and of the Son and of the Holy Spirit'

At the time of writing this testament, it could be practically anyone else talking in my place. These days everyone who is Lebanese, or lives in the Lebanon, is in danger. As one such person, I can see myself being kidnapped and killed on the road that leads to my village at Nabha. And just in case my premonition comes true, I am leaving a note to my family, to the people in my village and to my country. To my mother and sisters I say with great conviction: do not be sad or, at least, do not weep and mourn unduly; our separation, for however long it may be, will really only be short; we shall meet again, that is certain, we shall meet again in heaven's eternal home – that's where true joy is to be found and, if we are kept apart, sadness too. But have no fear, God in his mercy will reunite us all.

I have only one thing to ask of you: Forgive those who

killed me with all your heart, ask with me that my blood, though it be that of a sinner, may serve as a means of atonement (*fidya*) for the sins of the Lebanon; mingled with that of all the victims who have fallen, wherever they came from and whatever their creed. May it be offered up in payment for the peace, love and understanding which have vanished from this country and from the world at large. May my death teach men charity; may God console you, take care of you and guide you through life. Have no fear, I have no regrets for this world. All that grieves me is that you will be sad. Pray, pray, pray and love your enemies.

And to my country I say: 'People who live in the same house can hold different opinions without hating each other; they can be angry with each other without becoming enemies; they can quarrel without killing each other.'

Remember the days of charity and understanding; leave behind you those of anger and discord. Together we have eaten, drunk and worked, together we have offered up our prayers to the one God, and together we must die. My father's partner was a *metouali* (Muslim) whom I called 'Uncle Hussein'. I liked to call him that. They were partners for seventy-five years without breaking their contract or even keeping records. Remember how it was when often, if you were unable to borrow a hundred pounds off your own brother, you had only to go to someone in the village, be he Maronite, Sunnite or Druze and he would help you out. Everyone knows that, but sin makes us blind. Everyone must pray according to his belief and his conscience that God may stifle his anger and that the plans laid down by the leaders of this world may be reduced to dust on the soil of this country which should not be obliged to pay for their machinations with blood.

I shall not rest, even in heaven, while this situation prevails in the Lebanon.

Turn my funeral into an ordination day, not a day of interment and sadness.

Let Father Bethos celebrate mass at my burial, without the presence of numerous priests or any official announcement. And if Abou Khalil could make my coffin out of old wooden crates, that will suit me fine. No funeral reception. I hope people will forgive me . . . but no shots or gunfire; I am but dust, it is the power of God that will raise me to the life hereafter. That's how it should be.

People will talk, but that shouldn't matter to you. If they had one ounce of compassion in them, they wouldn't kill each other and let the wolves put us to shame . . . How wrong they are!

Let the choir sing as much as they like . . . that would give me great pleasure.

As I write, I am thinking of everyone, not forgetting any of my comrades and friends. My affection for them makes me want to find words of hope, and I think I have found the right message: 'Pray for me, fear God and love Him.' Always remember in your prayers those men and women who have committed themselves to the religious life as living witnesses to Christ come amongst us in this world, especially the Franciscans, the Jesuits and the priests from the Prado: it was through them that I came to know God, not to mention the material help they gave me.

As for what I must do, above all else I am a sinner . . .

I ask you all for your forgiveness, because I have sinned against you all. Take heart.

I, a sinner, remain yours through Jesus Christ, our Saviour.

Ghassibé, may your radiant death in the footsteps of Christ teach all of us, sinners, how greatly we must love.

8. Conclusion

My mother's rosary

As I conclude these pages, one beloved figure comes to my mind – my mother, to whom I owe the best in me. Left a widow at the age of thirty, with three children, she carried on her husband's export business quite competently. Somehow she managed to combine a father's firmness with a mother's tenderness.

I had just finished the first lap of my studies and dreamed of going on to university but my mother refused to let me: 'You are too coquettish and flighty. I have never seen you study seriously. You'll spend your time flirting.' I was fuming inside, but then if I was honest, what most attracted me to the idea of university – books or moustaches? (It was later, in the convent, that I would get my degree.)

Just to prove to everyone else and to myself that I did have intellectual abilities, I joined the best library and littered the house with volumes of literary works. I also went to very scholarly evening classes on philosophy. Tennis, ice skating, dancing . . .

I shall remember that historic evening all my life. 'Mother, it's a quarter to eight, I'm going.' Contrary to habit, that day my mother had already gone to bed, tired. She was holding her rosary in her hand.

'Goodnight, sweetheart, have you got your key?'

'Yes,' I kissed her and set out.

I walked down the street, but why didn't my feet take me in the direction of the college where the classes were held? Some sort of demon got into me. What adventure was I being lured into? I was walking along slowly, feeling dejected, when this character came up to me. I didn't react. He took my arm. I let him. I can't remember what he was on about, but suddenly he said to me, 'You look like a genuine sort of girl. What are you doing walking along slowly like that at night?' I felt as if I were at the bottom of an abyss unable to get out, suddenly stripped of all my will-power. I made up a story on the spot: 'My fiancé's left me.'

'Your fiancé's left you? Well now, there's a fine state of affairs . . . people quarrel, but they make it up afterwards. Come on now, go home, love.'

When I came to my senses I was outside the door of the college where the class had already started. The teacher was expounding the philosophy of Kant and its categories by a process of learned reasoning. I couldn't have cared less about it all. I jumped on a tram and went home. My mother had fallen asleep with her rosary between her fingers.

I have often thought since about that eventful evening, and I am firmly convinced that the beads of my mother's rosary slipped invisibly between that character and me. A voice was murmuring: 'Pray for us sinners, now . . .' and the man had said 'Go home, love' without knowing what he was responding to. In my gratitude, I have often prayed for that man. I shall seek him out in the next world to thank him.

How is it that, notwithstanding so many conflicting winds capable of uprooting mighty cedars, my poor little shrub is still standing? I know why. Its roots were strong. For as long as she was able, my mother went to church every day and took communion for her children. 'Do you really want to go into a convent?' she said to me. 'Then, be a good nun.' Every morning she sent me the necessary strength. How those ragpickers would have loved her; or rather, how she loves them! I know that she is there, in my smile which was on her lips as she passed away . . .

Thank you, God, for having given her to me for a mother.

Let's sing together

I can already hear someone saying to me: 'Your book is very fine, very edifying, a proper nun's book. But all the same, surely you're not going to tell us that what you have seen most of in your life, have been edifying things?'

'Do you think I live in a different world? Of course I've seen scandalous things, great and small. What about them?'

'What about them? Why don't you say more about them?'

Ah, my good friends, there we have it! It's all a matter of choice: when I stumble upon a dead dog in the street, or the guts of a pig covered with flies, I fix my eyes on the youngsters laughing and chasing each other in the distance. I have always preferred life to death.

I have to admit that it also has something to do with being contrary. My mother always used to say: 'You never want to do what everybody else does.' I subscribe to a magazine which reviews books and films (being lazy, a summary is quite enough for me) and I've noticed that they nearly all look on the dark side. It seemed quite impossible to have the unfortunate lovers united in the end. It's absolutely vital that one of them should die and the other commit suicide, or that, for reasons known only to the author, one should dive off to the right while the other disappears left. A few nice murders in the middle, some bed scenes showing every intimate detail, throw in drugs and drunkenness and thus the authors are guaranteed the finances for an expedition to the moon: our world has become so sad and so ridiculous that they have to launch themselves into some other orbit.

163

Just to be different, I focus on good people. As for the poor, weak, sinful characters — I'm forced to see their sort every day, every time I look at myself in the mirror.

Yesterday on the radio they were talking about a crime of passion and revenge in which seven people had died — they were strangled and flung in a cave. I looked at my little heart in the mirror and found a trace of black in it: someone had hurt me and I'd said to myself one day: 'How I'd love to strangle her!'

Fine! All that may well be true, but what then? Then I turn to Christ. Scoundrels laughed at the dying man they had crucified, and what did he do? He prayed: 'Father, forgive them, they know not what they do.'

So I take hold of that sad creature who looks so like me he could be my brother, and stand him at the foot of the cross next to those he has strangled, and I wait for a drop to fall and make us clean. Then afterwards I get to my feet . . . and give thanks to God as I sing the Magnificat. I, and many others in this world, haven't actually strangled anybody yet. You haven't either, my friend and reader?

In that case, come on — let's sing together!